GOTHAM BOOKS

GINA
GERSHON

In Search of
CLEO

How I Found
My Pussy

AND

Lost My Mind

GOTHAM BOOKS

Published by Penguin Group (USA) Inc.
375 Hudson Street, New York, New York 10014, U.S.A.

Penguin Group (Canada), 90 Eglinton Avenue East, Suite 700, Toronto, Ontario M4P 2Y3, Canada (a division of Pearson Penguin Canada Inc.); Penguin Books Ltd, 80 Strand, London WC2R ORL, England; Penguin Ireland, 25 St Stephen's Green, Dublin 2, Ireland (a division of Penguin Books Ltd); Penguin Group (Australia), 250 Camberwell Road, Camberwell, Victoria 3124, Australia (a division of Pearson Australia Group Pty Ltd); Penguin Books India Pvt Ltd, 11 Community Centre, Panchsheel Park, New Delhi–110 017, India; Penguin Group (NZ), 67 Apollo Drive, Rosedale, Auckland 0632, New Zealand (a division of Pearson New Zealand Ltd); Penguin Books (South Africa) (Pty) Ltd, 24 Sturdee Avenue, Rosebank, Johannesburg 2196, South Africa

Penguin Books Ltd, Registered Offices: 80 Strand, London WC2R ORL, England

Published by Gotham Books, a member of Penguin Group (USA) Inc.

First printing, October 2012

1   3   5   7   9   10   8   6   4   2

Copyright © 2012 by Gina Gershon

All drawings by Gina Gershon.

Gotham Books and the skyscraper logo are trademarks of Penguin Group (USA) Inc.

LIBRARY OF CONGRESS CATALOGING-IN-PUBLICATION DATA

Gershon, Gina.

In search of Cleo : how I found my pussy and lost my mind / Gina Gershon.

p. cm.

ISBN 978-1-59240-766-8

1. Gershon, Gina.   2. Women cat owners—California—Los Angeles—Biography.   3. Cat owners—California—Los Angeles—Biography.   4. Cats—California—Los Angeles—Biography.   5. Pet loss—California—Los Angeles.   6. Human-animal relationships—California—Los Angeles.   I. Title.

SF442.82.G47A3 2012

636.80092'9—dc23

2012006598

Printed in the United States of America

SET IN BAUER BODONI AND ARCHER

DESIGNED BY JUDITH STAGNITTO ABBATE / ABBATE DESIGN

CONTENTS

I have said that cats serve as Familiars, psychic companions. "They are certainly company." The Familiars of an old writer are his memories, scenes and characters from his past, real or imaginary. A psychoanalyst would say I'm simply projecting these fantasies onto my cats. Yes, quite simply and quite literally, cats serve as sensitive screens for quite precise attitudes when cast in appropriate roles.

· WILLIAM BURROUGHS ·

'Tis strange—but true;
for truth is always strange;
Stranger than fiction

· LORD BYRON ·

In Search of
CLEO

How I Found
My Pussy

AND

Lost My Mind

· CHAPTER ONE ·

The Set Up

S O I LOST MY CAT. Well, actually he was quasi-abducted by my hippy-dippy assistant Cassandra★, who grilled vegetables, taught yoga, and spelled her name with a star. She exuded positive energy, and I believed that all these attributes made her a responsible mammal. Unfortunately I was wrong. I had left Cassandra★ in charge to take care of my life while I was away in Cannes at the film festival. When I returned home from the trip, I learned just how wrong I was to leave Cassandra★ With a Star in charge of my life. As I walked through the door, all

I wanted to do was take off my Euro-wear and cuddle with my best friend of three years, my kitty cat Cleo. Cleohold, keeper of my heart, truth of my soul, my bud, my beast. He was Coco, Coco Puff in the morning, standing one foot, three inches on four paws. He was Spooky under the bed. He was Mr. Naughty when he was outside. But in my arms, he was always My Cleo.*

This cat had been through the ringer with me. In the last few months alone, my uncle Jack had died; my great friend Ted Demme, whom I had moved in with, had died; two other great friends of mine both died of incurable diseases; and I had just broken up with my boyfriend of eight years (who didn't die). Needless to say, I was in a pretty dark place.

So when I came through the door looking for my baby, my love, my support system and asked Cassandra With a Star, *"Where's Cleo?"* and she hemmed and hawed and guiltily responded, "Wellllllll . . ." I immediately felt my body begin to change. It was as though hair sprouted from the pores on my face and my fingernails morphed into claws, Wolfman style. A tsunami of rage was building within me, threatening to rip her hippy-dippy body into shreds.

By the time she confessed that she had wrapped

Cleo in a blanket and had taken him to the dog groomer—really, a *cat* to a *dog groomer*?!—steam was coming out of my ears. Who takes a cat to a dog groomer unless they are species challenged or a complete imbecile? To her surprise, Cleo got scared, wriggled out of the blanket, and escaped. *Run, Toto, run.* Not only had he run away, but he'd been missing for more than three days, and for some reason that defied logic, Cassandra★ hadn't bothered to call me. I pictured my hands, wrapped around her hippy-dippy throat, slowly choking the life out of her and burying the body in Cleo's litter box. I found my hands acting on their own accord, but thanks to the little voice in my head, that said, "Don't do that! She will sue!" I was able to pull back my reaching, stiff, angry fingers away from her patchouli-oiled hippy neck. Scared that eventually the beast within would win, I grumbled, **"Please leave, Cassandra★,"** my voice resembling Linda Blair's in *The Exorcist* after the demon had taken over. She stared at me, fear in her eyes.

"Please leave now, really! You must go before I kill you! I'M NOT KIDDING! GO!! I WILL KILL YOU. GOOOOOOO!"

But before she scurried away, the still human part of my being had the good sense to ask her where exactly she had lost my cat. And, thus, I began my search for Cleo.

The Beginning

It was a snowy morning and we were still asleep. For the past few days I had been talking about how it was time to get a cat. My boyfriend at the time and I had a place in Los Angeles in the hills with a nice backyard for a kitty. He said absolutely not. He stated very clearly that he did not like cats, and he certainly didn't want to live with one. Of course, I decided to ignore him completely.

Then one morning when we were in my New York apartment on 12th Street. (It seems like everyone at some point has lived on 12th Street.) It was one of those old brownstone buildings, and it shared a courtyard with my 11th Street neighbors. Even though I did not have direct access to the "backyard," my little one-bedroom had windows facing outside, and I had a beautiful oak tree that I would see as soon as I opened my eyes in the morning—a great luxury to wake up to in the middle of the city. It also felt safe, since our courtyard was protected by very high concrete walls.

This morning was particularly quiet, since there

had been a storm the night before and New York was blanketed with fresh white snow. I was awakened by what I thought was the sound of a baby crying. No, it was more like an animal whining. I looked out the window, and in the middle of all the white was a black spot. A little black spot crying out for help. As my eyes woke up and fully focused, I realized it was a beautiful panther-black kitty, with intense green eyes, staring at me and howling in a little kitty voice from the middle of the snow-covered backyard. I immediately opened up my window and quietly (so as to not wake up my sleeping boyfriend) gave specific directions to the scared kitty on how to come inside via my bedroom window. I pointed and whispered, "Go to the left, onto the table, jump to the slight ledge that leads to my window, and come inside. Hurry! It's cold!" The kitty listened carefully and then did exactly what I said. Before I knew it, the kitty leaped inside, right onto me, and starting kissing me like mad. It was love at first lick. We head-butted and snuggled for a good ten minutes before I told the kitty that she (I assumed for some reason that this feline was a girl) didn't need to sway me but had to convince my sleeping boyfriend to let her stay. Kitty looked at the sleeping boyfriend, then looked back at me with a smirk that said, "Watch

Cleo when he was a young and handsome panther.

this," and plopped herself down right on his head and proceeded to lick his face while pawing his cheek. It was a seduction that would have made Cleopatra proud. So when my boyfriend decided that this kitty was fantastic because she loved him so much (men are so easy that way), I decided to call this little seductress Cleo, short for Cleopatra.

Even though Cleo seemed to have fallen from the sky, I knew she must have belonged to someone in the courtyard; she was far too well kept to be a stray. I must admit, however, that in the many years of living there,

I had never seen this kitty before. I would leave for the day and put Cleo outside, expecting her to go home, but every night she would be at my windowsill, waiting to come in and love me. When it was time to go back to California, I said good-bye, expecting never to see her again. When I returned three weeks later, David Byrne, the singer of one of my favorite bands, the Talking Heads, and who happened to be one of my courtyard neighbors, said he and his family had put signs up, but no one had claimed the kitty. Cleo had waited for me every night on my windowsill to let her in.

"This is your cat. He belongs to you," he said in a simple yet truthful very David Byrne way. As he said that, I had the strangest sense of déjà vu, and I found myself nodding in agreement. I asked Cleo if she wanted to come to California with me. She said yes. I was psyched. Before we went, though, I took her to the vet to make sure she was healthy and to get all her vaccines and paperwork in order. Not only did I discover that Cleo was in fine form, but I found out that she was really a he. Cleo was a dude! I had gotten so used to calling "her" Cleo that I didn't want to change his name. Thus, Cleopatra officially became Master Cleohold.

So off to California Master Cleohold and I went to live up in the hills of Laurel Canyon.

CHAPTER TWO

Cleo Lost

CLEO AND I HAD BEEN together for around three years and had developed a very tight bond when Cassandra* lost him. So needless to say I was freaking out. It was as though my heart were wandering around somewhere in the streets of L.A. in the form of a black furry being, and I had to find it. The very next day I woke up at 4:30 in the morning, armed myself with a can of tuna and a knife (the tuna for Cleo, the knife for protection), and journeyed out into the flats of West Hollywood, in the vicinity of the infamous dog groomer. I thanked God it was the flats, because if it had been the hills, Cleo would have been coyote food.

I walked down the street, self-consciously yodeling, *"HERE, KITTYKITTYKITTYKITTY! HERE, CLEO! WHERE IS THE CLEO? YOU ARE NO GOOD!"* This is the cry I would always call to Cleo, ever since he was a little itty kitty. He recognized the yodel and would always come running to me, knowing that playtime was over, and feeding time was upon us. So from that day on, the tuna, the knife, and the yodel became part of my daily ritual.

This was Lonnye's "Lost Cat" poster that she made and later framed.

I put signs up everywhere, with a handsome picture of Cleo, and offered a reward to anyone who could find my lost love. I put ads in the paper, mailed out postcards with Cleo's furry face, and Lonnye Bower, my friend and Cleo's godmother, made T-shirts with his picture and the words "Got Cleo?" across the front. Lonnye had originally been part of my ex-boyfriend's regime. She used to help out in his office but soon began to help me with computer stuff, and since she loved cats so much, she often would take care of Cleo when we went away. After the breakup, she helped me and Cleo move into Teddy and Amanda Demme's compound, as it were, in West Hollywood. Lonnye and I remained friends, and she and Cleo loved each other, so after a while she was officially named Cleo's godmother.

It's a funny thing about breakups. You can be with someone for so many years and create an entire community of friends, really good friends, and then just like that, when you are no longer a couple, some of those "really good friends" just disappear from your life forever. It's bad enough that you are no longer with your ex, but you lose contact with a bunch of people you thought were important in your life. Well, fuck 'em. Truth be told, some of the ex's friends were a cynical and desperate bunch. I didn't really mind

Lonnye Blake Bower

The "Got Cleo?" T-shirt that the troops would wear

losing them. However, I did miss the warmth and coziness and safety of having what I perceived to be a home for the first time since I was a little girl. I thought this was my guy. From the moment we met, there was an instant recognition that we were supposed to be together. We even had chosen the same names for our hypothetical future kids. And I'm not talking Bill and Mary. These were very odd names.

It seemed like more than just a strange coincidence. (I know I should probably say what those names are, but I don't really feel like it. If you ask me in person I will tell you. Maybe. Probably not.)

When I was just twenty years old my father died suddenly of a massive heart attack. Just like that, his heart stopped, and in that very same instant mine split in two. Slowly and tenuously, time and the thread of life began to stitch back together my ticker, and I tailored a world that I could safely wrap myself back up in. Years later, when the *big* breakup came with my boyfriend who I'd been living with for the past eight years, it was as though the crack reopened and deepened into a crevice of sadness. Before I could mend this wound, my uncle Jack (a bit of a second father to me) died unexpectedly, filling that sorrowful crevice with a cement-like heaviness. I happened to be in St. Petersburg at the time, and luckily plenty of vodka was easily accessible. Thankfully, big protective Teddy was there with me to hold my hand all the way back to L.A., doing his best as always to make me feel better. This was something he was extremely good at. He would compassionately listen to me, throw up my sorrows and fears, and then eventually get me to laugh about something ridiculous. He even had the

Beautiful Ted at Dave and Anuschka's wedding on a beach in the south of France. Thus the flowers in his hair.

ability to make me believe that I would fall in love again, convincing me at times to "not worry," that he'd help me "find The Guy." Meaning the Right Guy. The Guy who would help me heal and make my heart smile again. Fill it up with emotional helium.

Then a few weeks after returning from Russia to bury my uncle, Teddy—like my father—died suddenly of a massive heart attack. I was devastated. The crevice had now widened into a gaping black hole of despair.

I literally, at times, was having a hard time breathing. I spent long, endless nights with only Cleo and the darkness, trying to fend off the unbearable, terrible anguish. Cleo would lay on my chest, over my heart, and lick my wounds, and oddly enough, it helped. And now Cleo was gone, too. Cleo, the only remaining piece of my heart that was still intact, was wandering somewhere, lost in the streets of L.A. I had no choice but to find him.

Imposter #1

After a couple of unsuccessful Cleo-hunting days, I was asked to be a presenter at the Tony Awards, which meant flying to New York. When it came time for the awards ceremony, I didn't want to abandon my search. Mara Buxbaum, my friend and publicist of many years, sweetly told me that I was starting to act insane and that I needed to please just get on the plane. I eventually consented and drove over to meet the fabulous Bob Mackie to borrow something to wear, and randomly, without hesitation, I gravitated toward a gorgeous long black beaded dress. Bob told me that it was the original black cat dress that he designed for the musical *Cats*. Coincidence? I didn't think so. Mara wisely talked me out of wearing the rhinestone "ears" as a headpiece.

As I was doing interviews backstage at the magnificent Radio City Music Hall for the awards show, I said into the cameras, *"If anyone in L.A. has seen my cat, please, please get in touch with me right away."* I think everyone thought I was joking. At least I got a laugh.

A few days later I was back home in L.A. and got my first call at two in the morning.

"Hey, I found your cat." My heart skipped a beat. *"I'll be right over."*

In my Ambien haze (I wasn't sleeping, so my sister insisted that I take sleeping pills, a common family practice), I drove over to some guy's house near Sixth and Sweetzer, hoping he wasn't a serial killer. He answered the door, and he was actually kind of cute, but I was there on business, so I focused on the blurry black cat that I thought *could* be Cleo. I was so desperate to get my loverboy back that I took this one home with me. I figured by the morning I'd know. Well, a girl can hope.

The next day I woke up to a stranger sprawled out on my bed, with this big, shit-eating grin on his face, like he had just won the lottery. He was flexing his paws. Licking his balls. He might as well have been smoking a cigarette. This fuzz ball was definitely not my Cleo. He reminded me of this production designer guy I had briefly seen who used to love lying around in my bed chain-smoking, pontificating about Nietzsche, Sartre, and Camus ad nauseam. Had this taken place during my angst-ridden college years, it might have been more interesting. Obviously he didn't last, and this imposter wasn't going to either.

Even Luca, the wild girl cat who lived in the backyard and was madly in love with Cleo, looked at me like I was an idiot once she got one look at this fraud. Poor Luca. She would wait outside my back door every morning with this look on her face like, "Bitch, go find my man." She would know the real Cleo even if she were blindfolded. From the first time she laid eyes on Cleo, she was in love. She would follow him around all day, and even though he would swat at her when she got too close, she would dutifully trail him wherever he would roam. A doomed groupie if ever I saw one.

And noting how young Luca was, no doubt Cleo was her first. Those of us who have been fortunate enough to know First Love know how intense everything feels. It's as though love opens up a secret portal to big, mysterious emotions and irrational behavior.

First Love

The first time I fell in love, I was seven years old. I was leaving the school Halloween carnival when a pale, skinny man with dark eyeliner and a cloak came up to me outside as we were waiting to cross the street. My mom was with me and talking to a friend of hers. It was unclear whether he was in costume or just an odd-ball Goth guy. Ever since *Dark Shadows*, the original vampire series, I had become obsessed and enthralled with the undead, and I was excited by the fact that he was a possible vampire. He was staring at me intensely (the way Barnabas Collins would stare at Angelique) as he held out this tiny little black-and-white kitten in his long, skinny white hands. My breathing became shallow and I seemed to be in a trance. Goth Man looked me deep in the eyes and in a very confident manner said, "This cat belongs to you. It is yours." I had no choice but to silently accept his gift with a quiet nod of understanding. He slowly turned and floated away. My mother, who had missed the entire exchange, finally turned to me and, seeing the kitten in my arms, immediately began to protest. I quickly reminded her that in my hysteria of Harry the Third's death (I'll get back to him later), she had promised me a new pet, and the goldfish that were swimming aimlessly around in the plastic baggie in my hand were mere decoration and didn't count. There was no negotiating. My future best friend and I went home to the safety of my pink-and-red floral room.

I decided to call him Kalookie—not only because I liked the sound of the name, but it also happened to be a cool card game. Kalookie didn't really trust anyone else in the house but me. For instance, he wouldn't eat anything until I got home. I would have to personally dish out his food, tell him how delicious it was, then stand over him before he would eat. Maybe he was poisoned in another life. He would also wait until I was in bed before cuddling up right next to my head to go to sleep. Like Xanax, his sweet purr would lull me right to sleep. If I got up in the middle of the night, he would, too, and follow me wherever I went. At times he felt like a watchdog, protecting me from any potential harm. If I was sick or crying, Kalookie would lick my hand and my face and not leave my side until I felt better. If I was feeling sad because my

My first love, Kalookie. Cleo would stomp on this photo whenever possible.

older brother and sister wanted nothing to do with me, he would sit on my chest and stare at me and make me feel important, like I mattered.

It was a very lonely period of my life as I recall. When the older kids would go out to do fun things, being forced to stay at home because I was "too little" brought out the anger and anxiety in me. It wasn't like the old days a few years back when I was four, and my sister would use me in her money-making schemes. My first paying gig was as a "spirit" who would hide out in the closet, wearing a bikini, until Tracy, dressed as a fortune-teller, would call out for the spirit to show itself and dance. In preparation for my "other worldliness" she would paint me head to toe in toxic, glow-in-the-dark paint and stick me under the lights until I activated. She would charge twenty-five cents per reading and would pay me only five a pop. Welcome to show business. At least I had felt needed and got to play with my big sister. But times had changed. It seemed like I was on my own. I seemed to be acting out a lot, getting into trouble and often ending up in the principal's office. I recently found a Valentine's Day card that I had been forced to make for this kid in my class whom everyone despised. A real know-it-all. He was always raising his hand, always having the answer, making the rest of us look bad. We all called him egghead. So when he was chosen as my "secret valentine," being an honest person, I made him a card that expressed my true feelings: a big heart made up of the word *shit* over and over again, with a big cursive *FUCK YOU* right in the center. Needless to say, I ended up in the principal's office once again, along with my parents, who were less than pleased and would have sent me to a shrink except for the fact that my father didn't believe in them. Truthfully, I think he just didn't believe in paying for them or anything else that he couldn't get wholesale. I was pleased that I got to keep the card. It was nicely done, albeit a bit aggressive (maybe they should have sent me to art school). As punishment, I was placed in solitary confinement, left to contemplate my actions. At least when I was isolated I didn't get into as much trouble, and it gave me time to consider how the Valentine masterpiece would look in a nice frame.

So now I had Kalookie. I would look at him and my heart would blossom with warmth and expansion. We were in love. I had his back, as he had mine. I guess you could say we had a bit of a codependent relationship. In some cases, I think codependency is good. So what if we wanted to eat all of our meals together? So what if I preferred his company to that of others who usually bored me? So what if he was my favorite creature on the planet and I wanted to spend all my time with him? I felt loved and wanted and always had a captive audience whenever I felt like performing a little song and dance. It was working for me! He even inspired my first love poem.

I have a cat Kalookie
And he is black and white

He sleeps in the doghouse
With my dog bandit all night
    [not true, but I needed a rhyme; never too young
    to understand the importance of poetic license]
His skill as a hunter
Was famous on our street
    [no one really gave a shit]
He catches lots of mice
Which he never, ever eats
    [just mutilated the fuck out of them]
I love Kalookie, and that is true
If I didn't have Kalookie
I wouldn't know what to do

It was an innocent time. A time when I used to swim or ride my bike simply because it was fun, not because it was exercise. When I ate a banana because I liked the taste and texture, not because it was "potassium." When I couldn't wait to get out of bed to start the day. (Now there are times when I can't wait to get back *into* bed to end the day!) Kalookie was always there waiting for me at home, with love in his heart and a purr in his throat.

My relationship with Kalookie showed how fierce I could be when it came to the ones that I love. One day, when I was around eleven, I came home and Tracy, my sixteen-year-old sister, was being a complete bitch. These were the days when she despised me, and having to share her room with her younger sister didn't help. But I thought she was the epitome of cool—she had really cute boyfriends, and she wore groovy, super-tight hip-hugger bell-bottom jeans. So what if I read her journals? I figured you don't write something down unless you secretly want it read. Besides, how else was I supposed to learn about blow jobs, partying, and other important teenage information that older sisters know about? Preparation is the key to life. She taught me that if you wanted to get a tan (remember, this was the Valley, so tans were crucial), you just pour a shitload of baby oil all over yourself, and if you really wanted to go for it, hold up some reflective tin foil to your face. She told me how the headband she wore was cool but that the piece of red yarn that I tied around my forehead, trying to emulate her, was just lame.

Well, on this one particular day, when I got home, she had locked our bedroom door and was playing "Smoke on the Water" really loud. I knocked, but she didn't answer me at first. Finally, by the time she yelled through the door to go away, I was getting pretty worked up. Not only was it my room as well,

Me, my mom, Tracy

and she was tapping into my repressed fury over being "included out," but Kalookie was inside, and I needed him. She said she didn't care and turned up the music once again. This was bullshit! I yelled to just give me Kalookie and then I'd go away. I just wanted my cat. We were screaming through the door back and forth and there was no way she was going to let me in. I could hear Kalookie crying for me on the other side of the door. Tracy turned the music up even louder. The driving DUM DUM DUM, DUM DUM DA DUM, DUM DUM DUM—DUM, DUM, DUM guitar riff was fueling my fury, and I suddenly felt this over-powering rage boil up within me. My kitty needed me, and with one final extra loud *"LET ME IN!"* I pounded the door so hard that my fist went flying right through to the other side and into the room. Then there was silence. My sister quietly opened the door and we both looked at the hole in amazement. With an air of dignity, and feeling like a badass, I waltzed right in, grabbed my cat, and strutted out with a newfound sense of empowerment. She would not fuck with me or Kalookie ever again, and over the years, this intense sense of protection over those I love got me into a bit of trouble here and there.

When Robert Buttface would not let my best friend, a now-crying Helen Gerber, get by as we were walking home, I found my hand balled up in anger, and even though I had never hit anyone before and he was a good foot taller than me, I yelled, *"You leave her alone!"* as my fist flew to the side of his head, causing him to let go of Helen's arm as his face turned beet red. Oh, shit! I grabbed Helen and yelled, *"Run!"* and we did. Another time a bunch of us were playing

"Schmeer the Queer,"* a tackle football–like game, a muddy favorite after a wet storm, and some eighth grader who happened to be a black belt went after my scrawny little surfer boyfriend, Eric. I pulled out a slingshot that would have made Dennis the Menace proud and threatened to hit him if he didn't leave Eric alone. Big mistake. This asshole tried out a few kung fu moves on me. When I was down on the ground, with the wind knocked out of me, I remember looking at him and in my best mafia princess imitation uttered, *"You are dead."* I ran home and told my big brother, Dann, what had transpired. This was right up his alley. We got in his 240Z and drove around the Valley until we found the Karate Kid. Dann rolled down the window and in a quiet Michael Corleone voice said, "Hey, Kung Fu! Come over here." The kid walked to the car, and my brother asked him to come closer. He made the mistake of sticking his head inside the car. Dann grabbed him by the hair and rolled up the window. He gave the car a bit of gas and looked him in the eyes. "You touch my sister again, and I'll take you for a tour of the Valley." Dramatic, yet effective. I never saw that douche bag again. Hey, this was the Valley, and we were little punks. We didn't know any other way. Survival of the fittest, as it were. And rule number #1: Always protect the ones you love.

Me as an adolescent badass. Notice the hip jut. Nice knee socks.

· CHAPTER THREE ·

Arthur

Aafter i brought the imposter kitty home, Lonnye and I had to put up posters of a FOUND black cat, next to the ones we had put up for the LOST black cat. Pathetic. As it turned out, the imposter's name was Mr. Lucky—boy, was he ever. His owners were thrilled to have him back. I hoped this counted as good kitty karma.

After the Cleo imposter fiasco, I went back to my daily routine. Up at 4:30, I'd get dressed in jeans, sneakers, hoodie jacket, and knife in pocket. I noticed my jeans were getting tighter. I blame the Ambien for that, which I seemed to be taking a lot of at that time. Not only would I wake up in a fog, but I'd have an empty bag of Milano cookies and random candy wrappers surrounding me in my bed, neither of which I recalled consuming.

You gotta understand that at 4:30 in the morning, L.A. is scary. No one's out. It's not like New York City, where there are still drunken party people walking home and hailing cabs at that hour. The Angelo streets are quiet, dark, and deserted. As I was wandering about, I noticed a beacon of light down the road. I walked toward it. As I got closer, I realized it was coming from a parked car, an old silver Honda hatchback, with newspapers spilling out of the open trunk. I noticed on the passenger's side a halo of golden curls—processed, golden Jheri curls to be precise. I couldn't see the lady's face that the curls belonged to, but I could see and hear her slowly filing her long-ass fingernails, back and forth, back and forth, back and forth. This woman's three-inchers put Cristal Connors's* nails to shame.

Suddenly, out of the darkness, a large man emerged. A big, black, slightly sweaty man. I should have been startled, but he had such a calming presence, with such a kind, beautiful, albeit moist, face, that I blurted out, *"I'm looking for my cat! You haven't seen any black cats running around by any chance?"*

"Ahhhh, you the girl with the posters all around? That your kitty?"

He was so sweet that I just nodded my head and started to cry. His massive arms engulfed me as he warmly hugged me.

"There, there now. Don't you worry, baby. We gonna find your kitty."

My father died far too young, and I missed him terribly. He was a gregarious giant who stood six foot five inches tall and weighed in at two hundred fifty pounds in his underwear. Every time a doctor would put Dad on a diet, Dad changed doctors. Ever since he died, I've always been a sucker for big men hugging me, telling me that everything was going to be all right. The big guy introduced himself as Arthur. I should have been afraid, but maybe it was an omen that things were going to be all right. Arthur was the newspaper man, delivering the news to the people, and this was his beat. I gave him my number and he assured me that he would call if he saw any lost black cats.

And the whole time, the lady in the passenger seat,

with her big ole head of glowing golden curls, never looked up. Not once. She just kept rhythmically filing those long-ass fingernails of hers. Back and forth. Back and forth. Back and forth.

As the weeks wore on, I saw a lot of Arthur. He was the only other person (besides his golden copilot) out at that hour. I would see him in the streets, and sometimes he would even call me up and enthusiastically say, "I spotted a black kitty! Come on down!" You couldn't help but love the guy. There was just something about him that made you feel good. Calm. I trusted him. He made me feel safe, and he always had good advice and little anecdotes that gave me a new perspective on life.

"Girl, you gotta live each day as though it's your last, and one day you'll be right." Or when I was letting the bastards get me down, he'd wisely tell me, "Child, don't let the 'lower' consume the 'higher.' "

He always seemed to be there to give me hope when I was feeling especially bad. He made me feel like I was not alone. His spirit reminded me so much of Marie—one of the most important people in my life and one of the constants in my childhood.

Marie

I was around two and a half years old when we first met, and she was the first black person I ever remember encountering. I was sitting at the kitchen table, with my head underneath one of those old-fashioned hair dryers that looked like a ready-to-pop Jiffy Pop popcorn contraption. My mother introduced us, and I took one curious look at this kind-hearted, dark-looking lady and said, *"How did you get so tan?"*

She laughed.

"I'z a Negro, child. I was born this way."

I took her hand and inspected it. One side was almost black; the other side looked just like mine. After thoughtful consideration, I had made up my mind.

"I'd like to be a Negro, too. How can I become one?"

"Oh, child, you tickles me."

Thus a friendship was born. Marie became my everything. She'd tell me stories of the South as she walked me home from school every day. She would bring me salted carrot sticks in aluminum foil so the salt would soak in, in the most delicious way. She made me fall in love with Southern food: grits, fried chicken, and collard greens, although I never went for the pickled pigs' feet, her favorite, which she would cook up as soon as my parents left the house.

"Eeewww, girl, I love me my pickled pigs' feet."

Anytime I was really upset I would run into Marie's room and cry and tell her what was going on. During those years, if my brother or sister saw me crying, they would taunt me and call me "baby," which of course made me cry even harder. Marie's room felt like a safe place to expose my tender emotions. She was also my faithful play date. We would watch the roller derby on TV, her favorite show, as she ate Cap'n Crunch out of a big mixing bowl and yell things like, "Whoop that white-ass honky!" I learned a lot from Marie. She was a badass from Rolling Fork, Mississippi, and I was a little Jewish white girl from the Valley. I loved her to bits.

She eventually moved in with us on a permanent basis. She had her own kids who lived in L.A., but she didn't seem to get along with them too well. Besides, they would make her pay to stay with them at their house. She had a good thing going with us. She took care of me, and I took care of her. I'd even run to the store to buy her NyQuil every other day.

"Geen, Geen, be a good girl now and run to the store to fetch me another bottle. My cough's getting worse."

I don't remember ever actually hearing her cough, but it seemed to make her happy, so I did it. She also seemed to have a bit of arthritis that would creep up every other week, especially when she had to comb and braid her hair. She would hand me this stinky, greasy goop and sit there while I lubed up her hair and carefully weaved a zillion bitty braids so they would smoothly fit under the wig she insisted on wearing. I would beg her to let me comb out her hair so it got really big and badass and she'd be all, "Girl, I can't be walkin' around with no 'fro! What's wrong with you?"

"What's wrong with me!? What's wrong with you?!" It seemed like a crime against nature if someone could rock a 'fro but did not. I guess you could say I had "'fro envy."

Marie even taught me how to play the Jew's harp. I had seen Snoopy playing the funny-looking contraption on TV—in some Charlie Brown special, of course—and was completely drawn to it. So when I saw one at Thrifty's, I decided to steal it. This was during my kleptomaniac years. I found the challenge of not getting caught thrilling. I stole everything from rubber balls to leather caps to the Led Zeppelin *IV* album. I would boldly stick items into my pants or confidently sneak them out under this nifty little woolen beige cape that my mother had brought me back from Mexico. So I stuck the Snoopy-approved Jew's harp into the pocket of my overalls, brought it home, put it up to my mouth, and tried to play. For those of you unfamiliar with the Jew's harp, it's an age-old mouth instrument that you place between your teeth and twang on the straight bit while creating a tone with the throat cavity. It kept clinking against my teeth, and blood and saliva starting dripping out of my mouth. And worse yet, the tone was awful. Marie grabbed it from me and said, "Child, give me that thing," and started making the craziest, grooviest sounds I had ever heard in my life. Supposedly she had played it on some plantation in the South, and she was obviously some kind of master. She called it a "Jew's harp" instead of a "jaws harp," as some call it. I figured, I was a Jew, so it must have been my chosen instrument. Eventually, with her help and guidance, I, too, became a master of the Jew's harp. This is the only thing that I will ever claim to be a "master" of. I'm proud to say I've recorded with several prominent artists—Christian McBride*, Rufus Wainwright, the Scissor Sisters, Leroy Powell*—and can even be heard twanging my harp on *Possibilities*, the

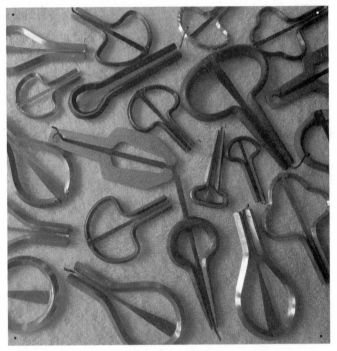

Some of my Jew's harps from all over the world

Grammy-nominated Herbie Hancock record (on the Paul Simon track). Thank you, Marie Gibson.*

By the time I turned sixteen, Marie had slowed down and decided it was time to move back to Rolling Fork, Mississippi, to be with her grandbabies. She had been with me for nearly fourteen years at that point. I didn't even remember life without her.

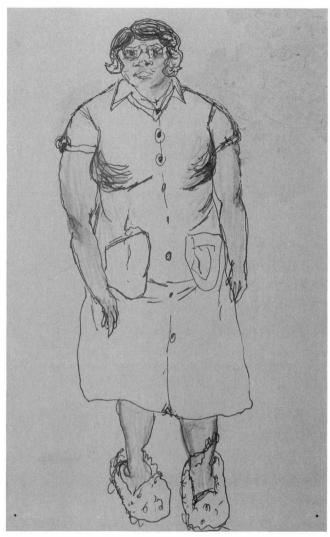

My Marie

I cried as she was leaving.

"You stay sweet now," she said with a final hug. And then she left.

I was "all grown," and there wasn't much for her to do but sit around and drink NyQuil. She called me a couple of months later and sounded happy to be back in the South. They had made her the "mother of the church," and she had gotten so fat that they "had to roll her down the street."

Not only did Marie provide a safe haven for me to express my most vulnerable feelings, but I definitely owe a piece of my soul to her.

Basically, I trust and like black people more than white people, especially when it comes to emotional matters.

Pimp, Pimp, Hooray

When I gave Arthur my phone number, I realized that if he were white I probably wouldn't have done so. Racist on my part, I know, but kind of true. For example, one of the best parties I ever went to was the Players Ball. I had become friends with the Bishop Don "Magic" Juan, Chairman of the Board of Famous

Players Everywhere. He used to be a pimp, but when I met him he was a preacher—and a stylish fixture among the rap-world elite. He's definitely one of the snappiest and flashiest dressers I've ever known. Not many people can rock a kelly green satin suit with matching hat and shoes, with just enough gold in the jewelry and accents to put a smile on anyone's face. ("Green is for the money; gold is for the honey.") He has been a kind and supportive friend, and I love how he ends each text and phone conversation with "Love you, baby, Church."

Anyway, I was his guest at the annual Players Ball, where they give out all sorts of awards to pimps all over the country. (I would bet that I was the only nice Jewish girl from the Valley there—or at least the only one who wasn't a hooker.) You've never seen such a colorful bunch. Elaborate fur capes and hats and shoes, color coordinated down to the fur collars and shiny alligator shoes. As I walked through, people would greet me with a friendly, "Hello, player." I guess because I was looking up as I walked through the ball, they knew I wasn't one of the hos. I was told that the hos traditionally kept their eyes to the ground. ("Pimps up, hos down," as the saying goes.) That part bummed me out a little for sure. . . . But the place was certainly hopping with energy and enthusiasm. "PIMP, PIMP, HOORAY!!!" was the chant that echoed throughout the makeshift ballroom located somewhere on Ventura Boulevard.

Some guy sporting a magnificent magenta and lavender fedora and matching double-breasted suit had the most amazing custom goblet I had ever seen.

"Oh, my God! That's so incredible!"

"Why, thank you."

"Where did you get it?"

"My friend makes them. He's out of Detroit. Would you like one?"

"Oh, yeah, that would be so great, I'd love one!"

I gave him my phone number and thanked him. My friend looked at me and laughed.

"What?"

"You just gave your number to this pimp that you just met. You don't even give out your number to people you know!"

Very true, I thought, but that pimp seemed like an honest guy to me! I had to deal with so many "professionals" in my business who really were just hos at heart. Why not have an honest-to-God pimp as my friend? That would be cool. Pimp, pimp, hooray!!!

Sadly, he never called.

· CHAPTER FOUR ·

Harry the Third

THE NEXT MORNING, as I wandered the streets looking for Cleo, I was feeling pretty down. It was chilly out, at least in the fifties—practically freezing for L.A.—and I'd forgotten to wear a jacket and was very tired. I sat on the sidewalk for a moment and tried to warm myself. Overwhelming feelings of sadness and loneliness came over me, and I began to cry and feel sorry for myself. Arthur appeared out of nowhere.

"What's wrong, sugar?"

"I don't know, Arthur. I just feel like a loser. I don't

have a boyfriend. I can't find my cat. I don't lead a normal life. I just feel pathetic."

Arthur sat down next to me. He began one of his inspirational pick-me-up speeches.

"You know, sometimes when something is lost, you find something even better. In order to gain something new, you've got to be willing to let go of the old thing. The old way. It's just how it is. Most of the time, the new thing is even better for you than the old thing. You just don't recognize it at the time."

Arthur's advice and golden words of wisdom always felt like simple little nuggets of truth. I bet he could make millions writing cards for Hallmark. Not only would he deliver worldly news to the neighborhood, but he could deliver the words of the heart to people all over the world.

Harry the Third suddenly popped into my mind, and I started telling Arthur all about my little golden duck.

Other than Marie, my only childhood companion was a duck that I named Harry the Third. Norman Klein was responsible for bringing Harry the Third into my life. He and my father were best friends, and our families would go on vacations together. Every Easter, to my delight and my parents' dismay, Norm would bring me a live animal for a present. One year it was a turtle (who mysteriously disappeared somewhere in the house, never to be found again). Another year it was a German short-haired pointer (who we named Spiro Agnew and who would chase our car for miles; he was eventually given to our cousins who lived on an avocado ranch, where he could run free and prosper).

But my favorite Easter gift was a tiny little duckling, who for whatever reason I decided to name Harry the Third. I guess I felt the title of "the Third" gave Harry an air of nobility and distinction.

I loved this duck. He would follow me around; our dog, Bandit, would follow Harry; and the little Chihuahua from next door would follow Bandit. I felt like the pied piper of domestic animals. I loved the fact that they would listen to my every word and obeyed me when I commanded them to *"STOP!"* Being the baby of the family by several years, I wasn't used to that level of respect.

Then one night my parents were having a dinner party. Marie had just finished giving me a bath. As soon as she zipped up my footsie PJs, I raced to the back porch so I could say goodnight to Harry. When I picked him up, his little neck flopped limply over to one side. I stared at him for a minute and couldn't figure out what was wrong with him. Marie came up behind me and solemnly said, "Harry's dead, child." I stared in disbelief and noticed that my five-year-old cousin was sulking in the corner. He was standing there, facing the wall, with his crew-cut pumpkin head guiltily peering over his rounded shoulder. "What happened to Harry?" I whispered, completely traumatized. My cousin shrugged. Sounding like Lennie from *Of Mice and Men* he complained, "Ducky no stand up anymore." Apparently he didn't realize the difference between a live duck and a toy duck and had attempted to wind him up by his neck, breaking it by accident. I freaked out. I ran into the living room where my mother and her friends were enjoying their pre-dinner martinis and began crying on her lap uncontrollably. My tears, snot, and drool cascaded down her hot-pink silk caftan. I remember thinking it was weird and kind of cool how my tears and snot turned the pink silk into this bloodred color. It was at this point that she calmed me down by promising me that I could get a new pet. And that's how I eventually got Kalookie.

Arthur contemplated the story.

"You see how that works, sugar? To get something new, something that might even be better for you than the original thing, you've got to let go. You may not see it now, but one day it'll all make sense. Have faith in that."

But I couldn't imagine anything being better than Cleo.

My sister, Tracy, with Bandit the dog, my brother, Dann, and me

CHAPTER FIVE

Magic Gay Cat

I SHOULD MENTION that Cleo has a few very specific characteristics that distinguish him from all other cats. First of all, he has a distinct mark in his mouth that he revealed to me when we first met. It's a perfect black dot on the roof of his mouth. I had been petting him, in awe of his poise and beauty, and asked him, *"Who are you? Where did you come from?"* He looked at me proudly, smiled, and did this sort of kitty yawn, tilting his head back so I could witness the perfectly round black mark on the roof of his pink mouth, like he was showing me the symbol of his tribe or something. It was impressive. Also, the way he drinks water is very unusual. He paws at the ground around the water bowl for a very long time, very horselike. And finally, his meow is very gay. Not the bruiser *MEOW* that one would expect from such a big cat, but a very high, sweet, twirly *bbrrow*. I would know his meow anywhere.

Anyway, I told my friends about my situation, about the "fake" Cleo that I brought home by mistake. Some of them said I should have just kept him. Others suggested that I get a new cat. Clearly these people were not cat people.

Look, if it's not the real thing, I'd rather be alone.

Now, let me clarify one thing. When I say, "cat people," I don't mean, like, "Oh, look at the nice kitty. I love kitties, and kitties love me." And I certainly don't mean the infamous Jocelyn Wildenstein* or the weirdo cat man who had all his teeth removed to install tigerlike dentures. What I mean is, I AM A CAT PERSON. Meaning, cats recognize me as one of their own. Let me tell you a little story, so you know exactly what I mean. . . .

Years ago I was up in Montpelier, Vermont, for the summer, doing a workshop with David Mamet while I was attending NYU. For those of you who have never been to this part of the world, Montpelier is a quaint little town, where all the roads seem to lead to the top of the hill where our school and dorm rooms were located. After five weeks with the same group of actors, writers, and directors, I was feeling a bit claustrophobic and had the need to just disappear—become invisible for a moment. I get this urge every so often, where I just want to get lost on my own, take off to nowhere, and not talk to or be seen by another human being for hours or even weeks. Get lost in order to find myself, so to speak.

Montpelier, however, is so small that those urges were always ruined by some friendly local stopping their car, saying hello, and offering me a ride. So, one night, when I needed to isolate, I snuck away from a restaurant where we had all been eating dinner. I decided that I'd have a quiet little walk home. I didn't want to deal with humans, so when I heard a car approaching, I would simply hide in the bushes until it passed. No big deal. When it was clear, I would resume my walk. After I had pulled off this little charade a few times, I sensed that I was not alone.

I heard a rustling in the bushes and discovered that this big orange cat was doing the same thing. A car would come, and we would hide. The car would pass, and we would nonchalantly continue our walk. The cat started walking ahead of me at a faster pace and would look back at me and start meowing, until I started to walk faster and match his pace. It's like he was saying, *"Hurry, hurry, hurry!"* He went down an unfamiliar street (we were practically jogging at this point) until we finally reached our destination—a small vacant lot, no larger than fifteen feet across, full of cats. There must have been thirty of them.

Oh, my God. He's brought me to a party with his friends! I'm like his date! That's so sweet!

I felt very honored, but as I stepped onto the lot, all of the cats looked up and started howling.

Oh, shit—maybe it's a human sacrifice ceremony! Not good. . . . I'm the only human here.

I started to worry until I realized that the cats weren't looking at me at all but straight up to the sky. I followed their gaze, and I swear I've never seen anything like it in my whole life.

The entire sky was filled with these crazy shooting stars, as far as the eye could see. I had heard about the amazing celestial activity in Vermont, but this was ridiculous. Obviously it was some kind of meteor shower. I looked up in amazement. The cats were howling, I was howling. I don't know if two minutes or two hours had gone by, but as suddenly as it began, it ended. The sky turned back to normal, and the cats became quiet. The show was over.

Everyone at the party started to leave. I was blown away. I looked for my date and found him rubbing himself against some other bruiser of a cat. A real stud muffin. These two hunky dudes were all over each other like two horny teenagers at an ecstasy rave. Was I simply a beard for my furry orange friend? Was there such a thing as a "gay cat"? Did cats even care about such a thing? Feeling like a third wheel, I politely interrupted the two lovebirds and said I had to get back. I had no idea where I was and needed an escort home. They kind of gave me a dirty look, but they rubbed each other good-bye and my date and I left the vacant lot.

I kept thanking my date for taking me to such a cool event and apologized profusely for breaking up the love-in. Like a perfect gentleman, he didn't complain as he walked me all the way back to the dormitory. After an awkward moment of silence, we said goodnight. No phone numbers were exchanged. No goodnight kisses were exchanged. Nothing. I never heard from him again.

CHAPTER SIX

Sonia

I WAS FEELING MORE and more alone. The only humans I was having contact with were the ones who would respond to my flyers, ads, television rants, and at this point radio shows. Yes, folks, I went on the radio to promote some acting project, but I abandoned the usual promotional riffing and turned the conversation to my lost cat.

People would call my house at all hours and say that they had seen my cat and that I should come over right away. I would get in my car and rush over with hope in my heart, and they'd be standing there with some mangled calico, and I would look at them, wondering if they were blind or just the by-product of immediate family interbreeding.

Amanda Demme was one of my dear friends who would join me every so often in the wee hours of the night, looking for our furry friend. We would pass long stretches of time reflecting on how different life was without Teddy around. As I mentioned earlier, after my breakup with my ex, Amanda insisted that I move in with her and Teddy. We had met exactly one time before that, on a crazy boat trip in Alaska, but we all fell in love with one another and immediately felt like family. So Cleo and I left the Canyon and began living in the modern glass house with the Japanese garden in the back of the Demme's main house in West Hollywood. It had cement floors, groovy chrome furniture, and a particular chair that Cleo loved. In fact, whenever Teddy would come over and sit in "Cleo's" chair, Cleo would get so annoyed that he would swat at Teddy's legs until Teddy had no other choice but to move over to the couch. Anyway.

Out of the blue one day, Ellen DeGeneres called me. In the previous few months, Ellen had become a good pal, and when I told her about my lost kitty, she accompanied me through the West Hollywood streets, mimicking my yodel, *"HERE, KITTYKITTY-KITTYKITTY! HERE, CLEO! WHERE IS THE CLEO? YOU ARE NO GOOD!"* She seemed to think the "you are no good" part was especially funny. "Why will he come to you if you keep insulting him?"

After hearing how desperate the situation had become, Ellen said in a matter-of-fact manner, "You need to speak with Sonia."

I didn't know who she was talking about, so Ellen proceeded to tell me all about Sonia, the animal psychic.

"Sonia's amazing. She totally helped me with my cat when he wasn't feeling well and was acting all depressed." When Ellen had moved to a new house, Sonia told her that her cat missed his old gray kitty condo and didn't like the new white one Ellen had purchased. Also, that the new wood floor had some waxlike property that was making the cat feel sick. As it turns out, Sonia was completely right. Incredible. She even had her own show, where she would figure out what was ailing animals, from horses to dogs to ducks. There wasn't a living animal with which Sonia couldn't communicate.

"Say no more." I called Sonia.

"H**I, SONIA. ELLEN TOLD** *me to call you. I've lost my cat.*"

"Yes, dahhhling, I know. He is very angry with you."

Please note that Sonia has a very posh English accent, which makes it sound as though she is exaggerating certain words while being annoyed with you at the same time.

"Yeah, I bet. . . . So, um, where is he, and how do I find him?"

"Well, before we get to that, there are a few particular things that Cleo would like you to know about."

"Okay."

"He says he doesn't just want you to give him the tuna juice anymore, but he wants to be fed all of the meat of the tuna as well."

Now this was a pretty good guess, because I would in fact sprinkle Cleo's dry food with a bit of tuna juice . . . and, no, I didn't give him any of the actual meat, but whatever.

"Okay. I can do that."

"Also, he wants to be fed in the old ceramic dish you used to use, not the metal bowl you use now. He does not like it."

"Ummmmmm. I never fed him in a ceramic dish. I've always used the same bowl."

"Yes, you did."

"No, I didn't."

"Yes, you did."

"No. I didn't."

"YES, YOU DID, AND HE WANTS HIS OLD CERAMIC DISH BACK NOW!"

Who the fuck was this woman? Then I remembered when Cleo first came to me in New York. . . .

"Do you mean the old Japanese ceramic dish?"

"Yes, dahhhling. That's the one. He would like to be served in that."

"Okaaaaay. Is there anything else Master Cleo needs before I go get him?"

All of a sudden it was like I was negotiating with Cleo's agent. Sonia then proceeded to tell me everything that had happened to me in the past year through Cleo's eyes. All of the loss, the breakup, the move, the cement floor that Cleo didn't like—he "prefers" parquet wooden floors. Okay, this was really starting to freak me out. The old house had parquet wooden floors, and now in the new modern pad, they were made out of cement. She was nailing everything. But the crazy part, the *craziest* part, is when she explained in detail the "two spirits" who were going to help me find Cleo.

"Dahhhling, there are two spirits that are going to help you find Cleo. The first is a man. I see him sitting down, playing piano. Beautifully. Music. There is a lot of music everywhere. . . . He is bald. . . . No . . . it's shaved. They shaved his head. Huh. He loves you very much."

I could feel my eyes beginning to well up. She was clearly talking about my Uncle Jack, who, as I mentioned earlier, had died a few months back. Not only was he an amazing piano player, but he was also an incredible composer and arranger. He wrote the music to *The Jerk* and *Where's Poppa?* and did the arrangements for *Blade Runner*, to name a few, and not only did he score the original "Charlie's Angels," but he wrote my favorite TV theme ever that bass players will love him forever for: *Barney Miller*. He definitely instilled in me at a young age a love for music. Since my dad died when I was twenty years old, Uncle Jack kind of became a second father to me. He was one of the coolest guys I've ever known. He died of a brain tumor, and they had to shave his head to perform the surgery.

"The second spirit is also a man." She started to laugh. "Oh! He's soooo funny! He makes me laugh! And he wears these big rings on his fingers. He's a big

My dad and Uncle Jack at a family dinner

man. Funny man! And he would sit in Cleo's chair! Cleo didn't like that at all. Oh . . . his heart . . . his heart hurts. He wants me to tell you, 'Don't worry. I'll help you find the guy.'"

Oh, my God. I started to sob uncontrollably. She was talking about Teddy. Not only one of the funniest guys I have ever known, and he did indeed wear big, bulky silver rings on his large, loving hands! And I know I have already mentioned the ongoing feud between Cleo and Teddy over the chair, and in fact he did have a massive heart attack at the all-too-unfair age of thirty-eight. But the real kicker was that he would always say to me, regarding boyfriends: "Don't worry. I'll help you find the guy." Sonia was hands-down the best psychic of all time. I *was* a believer, ready to do whatever she said. . . .

"Dahhhling, you must urinate in a jar. A Tropicana bottle seems to work best, because people will just assume it is apple juice. Then leave trails of urine going back to your house so Cleo can *smell* you and find his way back home. You must make sure you get down on your knees and see the world through his eyes. Oh! One more thing. He wants to be picked up in the limo . . . or you can pick him up in the big black car—you know the one."

In fact, I did indeed drive a big black Cadillac at the time. I could not make this shit up.

PEEING INTO A TROPICANA APPLE juice bottle is as messy and disgusting as it sounds. Maybe I should have used a funnel. I'm not good with pee, vomit, and other bodily fluids. I get totally disgusted when I have to pee for the doctor—the warmth of the pee in the cup totally grosses me out. I find the distinct smell repulsive, and I don't even like the color.

When I hear sex stories about people peeing and pooping on each other, I totally don't get it. Call me old-fashioned. Although I once read that Hitler was into being pooped and peed on. Maybe it's the Jew in me that finds this repulsive? Anyway. I had three empty Tropicana apple juice bottles lined up in my bathroom. The first time I tried it was a total bust. Pee ended up everywhere except in the bottle. It was getting really messy. If only I had a penis, it would have been much easier.

Once I finally had a full bottle, I had to figure out where to store it. The last thing I wanted was for my housekeeper or Teddy and Amanda's daughter, Jaxon, who randomly came into my house to play, to think, "Oh, yum, apple juice." What should I do? Label it? PEE: DO NOT DRINK (very *Alice in Wonderland*). People would definitely think I was losing it. I decided to put it in my cupboard until I was ready to use it that night. I really hoped it wouldn't smell up the joint.

CHAPTER SEVEN

Hell's Angel

THE LOCALS STARTED GETTING USED to me wandering through their streets yodeling, *"HERE, KITTYKITTYKITTYKITTY! HERE, CLEO! WHERE IS THE CLEO? YOU ARE NO GOOOOD!"* I made sure to keep the knife out of view. I think that would probably have made them nervous.

It was 6 A.M. and I was crawling around on my hands and knees in some backyard, trying not to get pee on myself, as I dribbled a trail of my urine out of the Tropicana juice bottle just like Sonia suggested. I was trying to see the world through Cleo's eyes, trying to figure out which way a kitty such as he would wander. There was a lot of weird shit on the ground. A teeny, tiny plastic doll that might have once danced on top of a chocolate cake. A dead blue balloon. A ripped-up old Monopoly card. A Mr. Potato Head sans eye and nose. A broken M&M doll. Either they had just had a kid's birthday party, or whoever lived here was a slob. Suddenly the backdoor swung open and there was a big, brown, angry-looking lady, hands on hips, schmatta on her head, yelling at me.

"Whachu doin' in mah backyard?"

I think her accent was Haitian.

Busted. I guiltily looked up at her. She paused for a minute, cocked her head, and asked, "Aren't you that lady from *Showgirls?*"

I nodded meekly.

"So . . . WHACHU DOIN' IN MAH BACKYARD?!"

Every day after that I expected to see my face on the cover of the *Enquirer*: "Confused Actress 'Marks Territory' in Angry Neighbor's Backyard!"

So I just turned and got out of there. *"HERE, KITTYKITTYKITTYKITTY! HERE, CLEO! WHERE'S THE CLEO? YOU ARE NO GOOD!"*

After I slinked away, I decided to pick up a hot pastrami sandwich to eat while I walked the streets.

As I made my way down this one road, kind of grimmer than the rest, I noticed an older man with wiry hair and broken glasses staring at me, suspicion in his eyes, while he took out his garbage. I had noticed him before. He lived in a relatively small putty-white house that only had one little window, and it was all boarded up. He never spoke to a soul as far as I could tell, but every day he had five or six bags of garbage that he placed on the street. I'm talking the big, black, Hefty-sized garbage bags. Every day! Who has that much garbage? I thought that maybe he was chopping up people he had killed, getting rid of them the old-fashioned way. After a few weeks of no eye contact, no nods of hello, no acknowledgment whatsoever, he waved me over. I cautiously walked over to him.

"You're the girl with the lost cat?"

I cautiously nodded.

Then he leaned in conspiratorially.

"There's some Afghanis around the corner. I bet they have it. But be careful, those Afghanis are dangerous."

He told me that he served in World War II and that he never got sick because he took ice-cold showers every day.

"Keeps the germs away."

He recommended that I do the same. I noticed him

glance over to the pastrami sandwich in my hand and wondered if he thought it had germs—or perhaps he was just hungry.

I nodded and thanked him for the good advice. He rambled on about germs and bacteria for a bit more, and, being a bit of a germaphobe myself, I listened very carefully. This guy didn't really look old enough to have served in World War II—he was probably sixty at the most—but I thought it was best not to question him. He decided to introduce himself.

"I'm one of Hell's Angels."

"Oh. Are you friends with Willie Nelson?"

"No. Not that kind of Hell's Angel. I'm an Angel. From Hell."

"Really? Huh. Well . . . that's cool." How does one respond to that?

I guess we established some sort of bond, and he began to trust me a bit more, but not totally. He very carefully positioned himself and started asking me questions, an investigative litany, and my reply would be the conduit to trust and respectability.

"Do you think it's better to be an angel in Hell or a devil in heaven? A rich girl in a poor world or a beggar in Utopia? A ballet dancer at the rodeo or a cowboy at the opera?"

I felt that our budding friendship depended on my answers, but I didn't have any that seemed worthy of the questions.

"Ah. Those are good ones. I usually go for the 'Would you rather be eaten by a great white shark or burned at the stake?' sort of thing. Or how about, if you could either fly or become invisible whenever you fancied, which would you choose?"

He stared at me blankly.

"Would you rather be a blind man in a kaleidoscope or a rainbow on a grave? The best of the worst? Or the worst of the best? An A in hypocrisy or a Fail to even take the test?"

Okay. He was either a raving lunatic or some kind of genius. Sometimes the two go hand in hand, I suppose. I must have waited too long to answer, because even though I appeared to be thinking quite seriously about his questions in a very respectful way, he slinked back into his windowless hovel.

The next morning when I saw him, I offered him half of my pastrami sandwich. (I was eating a lot of pastrami sandwiches during this period. I'm not sure why.) He carefully told me that he couldn't eat it, but he did not judge me.

"To be a meat eater, you have to be able to look at a

cow or chicken, or even a fish for that matter. You have to be able to look them straight in the eye and be able to say, 'I just ate your daddy.' If you can do that with a clear conscience, then you will have no problem defending your carnivorous ways. I'm just not that guy."

Respectful silence. I suddenly felt very self-conscious about my sandwich and very casually hid it behind my back as if it didn't exist, hoping he would forget I even had it.

He started reminiscing—as much to himself as to me—about his great love from his past.

"She was my other half. My soul. My enema."

"You mean your anima?"

"No, my enema. She cleaned me out and purified me."

Huh.

"Let me tell you something, girlie. Life's a roulette wheel. You just spin it, and who knows what number you land on . . . unless, of course, you *know* the number you want to land on. Do you know what your number is?"

Roulette wheel. Gambling. Now we were talking about something I understood. I told him about Norm Klein. Along with my father, Norm, the one who gave me Harry the Third, taught me the art and rewards of gambling. We would play backgammon and liar's dice, and when I got up to a hundred dollars in winnings, Norm would take me to the track and show me how to handicap and bet on the horse of my choice. I enthusiastically explained to Enema Man how my first bet was on a horse called Lover's Fool at Hollywood Park. The jockey who was riding him, Pincay Jr., happened to be one of the best jockeys around, and, more important, I liked the colors he was wearing. He won the race, and I was twenty bucks richer. Positive reinforcement via Lover's Fool. Thinking out loud, I stated that this must have been an omen for most of my romantic life.

He looked at me with what I think was a tinge of disappointment, or regret, in his eyes.

"I strongly suggest you choose a different number."

Hell's Angel

CHAPTER EIGHT

Booty Cat

AFTER THREE WEEKS WITH no luck, I started getting depressed. Really depressed. Everyone around me was starting to get seriously worried. So I did what everyone else was doing: I started taking antidepressants. Wellbutrin, to be precise. After a few days, it kicked in and definitely helped. My nighttime excursions weren't as tortured. I passed the lonely hours remembering past relationships—the good, the bad, and the ugly—and I fantasized about what and whom I would've done differently.

The Writer: Brilliant, "eccentric," and intellectually challenging. I learned that crazy is fun to visit, but you don't want to live there.

The Actor: Spontaneous, sensitive, deep, and passionate, but there was not enough room in the mirror for the two of us.

The Viking Guy: Tall, hot, interesting, and dumb. Hands down the most self-centered person I had ever met. Projection is a misleading thing. He wasn't interesting at all. Once the magic wore off, it was as though I was staring into the face of dumb. Sometimes it *is* appropriate to judge a book by its cover.

The Billionaire: Fun, extravagant, and too needy. He basically wanted me to give up my career to become a Stepford socialite—too high a price to pay.

The Surgeon: He helped rebuild children's cleft palates so they could smile—very noble, but this guy turned into a serious stalker and wiped the smile right off my face.

The Rock Star: Need I say more? Oy.

All I wanted was a nice, funny, smart, successful, generous, interesting guy who was passionate about what he did and not annoying to be with. Was I asking for too much? Apparently so.

The closest I had come to this was with the ex-boy-friend who I had just broken up with at the beginning of this story. This guy had it all. I thought I was going to marry him, have his children, and live happily ever after. That is, until he had some sort of psychological breakdown and became incredibly depressed. I tried my best to help him, but let's face it, you can't help someone who is unwilling to help himself. After many months of trying, he gave us no choice but to break up. Not one of my finer moments. Not a good-time memory.

Finding the right guy, I've decided, is like finding that perfect pair of boots. You rarely find them when you go out looking for them. Try as you might, there's always something slightly off. The heel makes you feel wobbly, or the height isn't exactly right. Or they may look amazing but are so uncomfortable you want to kill yourself by the end of the night. If it's not the whole package, it's better to go without. And if you are not careful, you talk yourself into believing that this is the one you have been looking for . . . and you end up with a closetful of frustrating boots that you have to throw out or give away to the next hopeful victim. But every once in a while, on that occasional blue moon, you come across the perfect boot. The kind you've al-ways dreamed of, the kind you could wear anywhere, the kind you know would make you happy . . . and of course, they are on someone else's feet, or out of stock, and have been unavailable for years.

"I found Cleo!"

I had been in New York for a few days when I got the call from Lonnye. She sounded excited.

"I'm pretty sure it's him. He came to me when I called out to him, and he totally looks like Cleo, so I brought him home, and he's eating and purring and licking and went right to sleep on your bed! I think it's him! I really think I found him!" I love Lonnye. I love that she was as invested in finding Cleo almost as much as I was. They have always loved each other. "When are you coming home?"

"Tomorrow."

"Shit. Okay. I have to leave in the morning, but I'll feed Cleo and leave the door open. I'm going into the desert for the weekend, so I'll be unreachable. But I know it's him! I'm sooooo happy! I'll come over on Monday, okay?"

"Sounds great. Thank you, Lonnye. You have been so incredible throughout this whole thing, and I really appreciate it."

"Of course. He's my godson. I love him."

I hung up the phone. My heart was pounding, but

I didn't want to get too excited just yet. But Lonnye would know Cleo. It had to be him. I couldn't wait to get home and shove my face into his fur.

The next day when I walked into my house, I was beside myself with anticipation.

"Hellllllllloooooo . . . where's my naughty boy?"

Nothing. I went upstairs, and lo and behold there was a black cat sleeping soundly on my bed. I put my things down and went over to give him kisses, but as soon as I touched his fur, as soon as I saw the whitish hair coming out of his ears, as soon as he lifted his head and smiled at me, . . . I knew it wasn't Cleo. Ugggghhhhh. My heart dropped along with my body onto the bed. Fuck! I was so tired of this shit. The fake Cleo licked my hand. He was a sweet boy. I pet him, and he licked me. I pet him some more. I looked him straight in the eye and said, *"Look, bud, you and I both know that you are not Cleo. You just happened to get lucky when you found Lonnye and tricked her into taking you home. Glad you've had a nice time, but now you have to go. You are cute and all, but I want my real guy back. Sorry."*

I put him outside, wished him luck, and went on about my business. I went through the routine of the day in a joyless, robotic way. I felt lonelier than before.

The disappointment of yet another fake Cleo took out another little chunk of my heart. Later that night, as I was getting ready for bed, it was so quiet. I usually love the sound of silence, but this time it just sounded lonely. I tried not to panic. Then I heard a noise. A scratching at my glass front door. It reminded me of one of those scary stories where the dead guy is hanging upside down from the tree, scratching at the rooftop of the car with his dead, dangling hands. I grabbed my knife and wandered over to where the noise was. As I got closer, two small globes appeared, glowing in the dark. The scratching stopped, and out of the darkness came a one-syllable *mrow*. It was him. The fraudster. I opened the door and he pranced in, and, I must admit, he was pretty hot and fully aware of his studliness. He strolled over to me, sniffed me up a bit, and showed off his strut as he made his way up to my bedroom. He jumped on the bed, expecting me to follow. This was one cocky motherfucker. I hated to admit it, but the idea of sleeping with a warm, cuddly body, even though it wasn't Cleo, just for one night, was very appealing to me at that moment. I was feeling weak and vulnerable. And he was supercute. What's a girl to do? I went to him and laid it on the line.

"Look, pal. You are not my guy. We both know that.

But you want something. I want something. And as long as we are clear that this is just what it is, you can spend the night. This is NOT a relationship. You are not moving in. This isn't going to last. You must leave in the morning. I don't need to know your family history. I don't care what you like to eat. I don't want to know which Elvis Costello album is your favorite. This is what it is. No gifts. No expectations. No worries."

I got into bed and the stud muffin started rubbing up against me, licking my hands and face. He was sweet and gentle and had a very seductive purr. He loved on me in the sweetest way, and at some point I fell asleep, warmed by his heavy body and yummy fur.

When the morning came, he kept up his side of the bargain. He was out of there. No "Thank you." No "Oh, I had a great time." No "I'll see you later." Just gone. I felt like we both got what we wanted, so why feel sad or used? Equal opportunity. I felt a tinge of guilt when I thought about Cleo, but I decided not to go there.

The next evening around midnight, I heard the same scratching at the door. My secret loverboy was back! He pranced in as though he owned the place, again not saying much. No "How was your day? Are you hungry?" No idle chitchat for this lothario. So I just turned off the lights, got into bed, and gave him what he came there for. In the morning, he was gone.

And so we became each other's booty call. He was my Bootycat, as it were. No obligations. No phone calls. Just my sleepover cuddle buddy. But then things started to change.

He started showing up during the day. A booty call no-no. At first he brought me a dead bird and laid it at my feet. Not quite chocolate, but a sweet gesture nonetheless. I kindly thanked him but sternly told him that I really didn't want him to bring dead animals into the house. We took a nap and then he left.

A few days later I was taking a lovely bath when I heard my special kitty friend make his presence known with a proud *meow*. I got out of the bath, and as I avoided stepping on him (he was right where I would put my feet), I saw this very frightened baby hamster looking around for an escape route. My paramour kept the hamster in line by swatting at him so he remained in place and didn't screw up his special presentation. The hamster looked at me with pleading eyes, and if he could have squeaked, "Help me," he would have. At least my gift wasn't dead, but I was really starting to get annoyed. I said to Bootycat, *"Listen, not only do I not want you to kill any animals on my behalf, but I don't want you to bring live animals into the house! It's just not cool."*

So then I was running around, naked and dripping wet from the bath, trying to coax the frightened hamster into a box so I could save him and release him back into the wild. That took a good twenty-five minutes, and I was pissed. I reprimanded the now-sulking cat some more—kind of our first fight—and he blankly stared at me and then took off like a shot. No love. No nap.

I, however, was exhausted from the early-morning Cleo excursion and desperately needed a disco nap before I went out for the evening. I was too tired to even walk upstairs, so I decided to crash on my couch. There was a nice Santa Ana breeze coming through one of the open doors, and I was out like a light. It was habit at this point to keep my downstairs door open a crack all the time during the day so Cleo could go in and out as he pleased. In my slumber I heard a low, growly sound. It seemed like the background dream sounds of a horny caveman in the middle of the night, trying to gently wake his woman. As the sound persisted and became more urgent, I opened my eyes— only to find my Bootycat hovering over me, grumbling in some primitive cat tongue.

Before I could say, *"What's up?"* he dropped something onto my lower stomach. My eyes popped open
just in time to see this huge *live* lizard scramble up
my naked body, looking for an escape route. Needless
to say, I screamed and jumped off the couch. The cat
screamed out of fear and ran to the far corner of the
room! Who the fuck knows where the nine-inch lizard went to—and truthfully, I didn't care, as long as
he wasn't still crawling up my bare body.

*"Are you fucking kidding me? What do you think
you are doing?"* I couldn't deal with this anymore.
"You have gone too far! I'm done! No more!"

Sure, I was upset and acting out of fear and emo-
tion, but let's face it, loverboy had broken the essen-
tial laws of the booty call. He was getting clingy and
needy and not respecting my needs or boundaries. Yes,
if this were a normal situation, maybe we could have
had a conversation about stepping up the relationship
to dating status or whatever. But come on. This guy
was hot and too well fed to be completely single. He
was stepping out on someone who was clearly taking
care of him, wondering where he was going when he
disappeared all night. Not the kind of disloyal guy I'd
want to have a relationship with. And this could never
extend to a "friends with benefits" scenario. I knew

NOTHING about him. Hardly someone I could consider a friend. No. It was over, and we both knew it. C'est la vie, as they say in the Old Testament. Too bad. It was nice while it lasted, but now we glared at each other with suspicion and anger instead of longing and curiosity. Why must it always end this way? He stared at me, unblinking, for a few more moments, and then with a flip of his tail, he turned and walked out of my life forever.

I never heard from him again.

CHAPTER NINE

Desperate Times, Desperate Measures

A T THIS POINT, SEVERAL WEEKS in, I was definitely living in my own little world. A friend of mine suggested that I see his psychic, Doris, who had been very helpful to him in business. In New York, everyone has a shrink, and in L.A., everyone has a psychic. I figured, "What have I got to lose at this point?" And to be honest, I was disappointed with Sonia's results. All that pee for nothing. I was willing to try anything, so I drove out to the Valley to see Doris. I was driving around, looking for her house, thinking how much the Valley had changed since I lived there as a kid. All the vacant lots had been replaced with ugly condos. And all the pomegranate and orange trees had been superseded by fast food joints. Finally I located her house, a boxy, beige, cookie-cutter prefab.

"He ain't comin' back!" were the first words out of her mouth. I literally burst into tears.

"How do you know that, Doris? How can you be so sure? You don't really know that, do you? I'm sure you've been wrong before. You shouldn't just say something like that, because you don't REALLY KNOW!"

I sobbed hysterically.

She put her cigarette out and very calmly said, "I guess I could be wrong . . . but I doubt it."

I continued to sob. In an effort to shut me up, she offered to send me to *her* guy.

Maybe he could help.

So I went to Doris's minister, and even though I'm Jewish, he said he would pray for me. He told me that I should come back on Sunday and pray with the entire church. I've never been that into organized religion, but I was willing to do and see anything and anyone

Doris the Psychic

who would give me hope, which was how I eventually ended up with the Santeria guy.

My friend, a highly revered guitar god, told me about him, made a call, and went with me to meet his "father." He needed to make the introduction in person, especially since my friend spoke Spanish and I did not. "Father" was this lovely little Cuban man who didn't speak a word of English. He had helped my friend through hard times by reversing evil spells and by helping him achieve his dreams. Santeria, for those of you who are unfamiliar, is basically a system of belief that merges Yoruba religion with Roman Catholic and Native American Indian traditions. After we did the initial chanting and throwing of these little rocks, during which he would read and nod his head and mumble to himself, he decided to take me on, and we set a date.

I picked him up at his apartment and we were to drive to Griffith Park at sundown. On the way, just a few minutes later, my Cadillac ran out of gas. Did I mention he lived in the heart of South Central? Not exactly the place you want to run out of gas in your pimped-out Cadillac. I pretended that everything was cool, and in my best seventh-grade Spanish said to the calm little Cuban, "Uno momento, por favor." I got out, went to the back of the car, and begin to push. Cadillacs are heavy. Luckily, some nice strong kid came to my rescue and helped. There was a gas station a few blocks away. I was dying. Here I have this little old non–English-speaking priest-father-guru guy just sitting in my car, acting as if nothing was going wrong, while this kid and I were frantically pushing the car down the street. Padre was one serene dude, I'll give him that. As we were pushing, I kept hearing a thumping sound coming from my trunk. The Santeria guy had put his bag in there before we left, but I couldn't imagine what the noise could possibly be. Whatever. I was just thankful when we got the gas and could continue on our mission.

When we got to the park, he took me to this remote area. He started chanting, drawing stuff in the dirt. Then he reached into his bag and brought out a cigar and a bottle of rum. He lit the cigar and had a swig of rum, then he spat the alcohol all over my face! Whoa, I didn't see that coming. He continued to do this, in between blowing puffs of cigar smoke into my face. Pretty fucking rude, I thought. But I just went with it. I kept thinking of Cleo. Then, just as I was getting ready to protest, he whipped out a knife. *Oh, shit.* We were in an abandoned area, and it was getting dark. What the fuck was I doing? And then he reached into his bag and pulled out a LIVE chicken! (Ahhhhh, *that's* what the thumping was in the trunk.) And then he proceeded to hit me with it! Hitting me all over with a squawking live chicken! Then, without any warning, he took his knife, slit the poor chicken's throat, let the creature's blood flow into the earth, and then buried it. Needless to say, I was a bit worried, but I thought it best to pretend that everything was Kool and the Gang. Don't show him any fear. It seemed the appropriate thing to do. Hopefully the guy wouldn't kill me. Okay, I really wanted to find Cleo, but enough was enough. He chanted a few more ditties and then calmly motioned that it was time to go. Thank God. Gracias, Señor Padre, gracias. I quickly drove him home and never contacted him again. Better not to push my luck. I felt so guilty, I didn't eat chicken for a month.

And then there was this other man, who looked like Santa Claus's nerdy cousin and who channeled a ye olde English–sounding guru and would give talks on everything from getting in touch with your inner child to how to have a successful relationship. My friend who collected and sold beautiful crystals was an avid follower of this man and informed me that he was holding a workshop over the weekend on the "lost city of Atlantis" and that I should go. I figured if he knew so much about a lost city, perhaps he could advise me about a lost cat. Listen, I've always been interested in cults and religions and the strange stuff people are willing to believe in order to get them through the day. I've just never really been a practitioner of any of them.

But desperate times call for desperate measures. I felt like one of these systems had to work. At this point, if someone had told me that sitting on a purple ball and chanting "zippity do da" five hundred times a day would get my Cleo back, I would have done it.

The weekend workshop cost five hundred bucks per day, and *hundreds* of people were there, clutching on to their crystals, nodding, and going "hmmmm" at this guy's every word. Every so often, spontaneous dancing would occur. I must admit, everyone seemed so joyful and free that I felt a bit envious. Had I become cynical in my old age? Had I become too self-conscious? Or had I simply missed the free Kool-Aid that they were undoubtedly handing out somewhere? I tried to focus. After Santa Claus lectured for about thirty minutes, there was a meditation. After a good long while that felt like forever, he asked if anyone would like to share. An overweight white woman with frizzy hair and a rainbow scarf eagerly raised her hand.

"What did you see?"

"I was in a big room. There were lots of candles."

"Was it beautiful?"

"Uhhh . . . yes! Very beautiful. Like a church."

"Was it a crystal church?"

"Ummmmm, yes. It was a crystal church! A church made out of crystal!"

"How did you feel?"

"Well, I . . . ummmm, felt . . ."

"Good? Calm? Like you were safely back in the womb?"

"Yes! I felt so good! And safe! I was very calm! Like I was back in the womb!"

Okayyyyyy. I tried not to be negative, but this was a group of suckers if ever I saw one. Almost as bad as the group in Palm Springs that I joined for yet another enlightened weekend in hopes of gleaning any sort of insight into the whereabouts of my lost love. I figured Palm Springs is the desert. Historically speaking, a lot of heavy things went down in the desert. Just ask Jesus. Maybe the Holy Spirit would lead me to Cleo.

One of my closest friends, and a *very* intelligent person, mind you, was totally into this "magical man" from Sri Lanka. My friend and his wife were both going to the weekend seminar in Palm Springs and suggested I come. Why not? It couldn't be weirder than any of the other things I was doing. I think I was secretly getting addicted to going to see strange people do strange things. Maybe it made me feel better about my situation? If I were in touch with some sort of spirituality, perhaps it would be easier to discover the path to Cleo. Perhaps he would just "appear" before my eyes. Who knows? Who cared? I went. People from all over the world paid *thousands* of dollars to get enlightened by this Deepak Chopra wannabe/ Houdini character who would blow light into your eyes that would magically appear from inside his mouth, so you could realize all the glory in the universe. I'm not making this up. And I really *wanted* to believe him, but my curious mind couldn't stop asking Sri Lanka man questions. What exactly does the "light" mean? How did it help people find themselves? How would it help me find my cat? He just smiled and said, "Gina, Gina, Gina," and then he suggested that perhaps I should become his assistant. Why? Because I was onto something? Because I was onto him? The whole thing seemed like a waste of time (not to mention money). I should simply get back to the streets to search. Keep making phone calls. Keep calling the local kennels, and, most important, keep my hopes up.

Someone told me about a manifestation technique. At night before I'd go to sleep I would try doing these "creative visualizations" of hugging and kissing Cleo. It reminded me of those sense-memory exercises that

I learned in acting school. I would pet his fur, feel the softness along my hand and face. I smelled his mouth. (I love the way his breath smells. Like sweet tuna with a tinge of leather boot.) In the visualizations, he would lie on my stomach and his purr lulled me into a relaxed state of being. His weight upon my body. The warmth of his body. I felt love. I felt coziness. I didn't feel alone.

One night I fell asleep without the aid of Ambien or Xanax. This visualization technique was really quite relaxing. It was a deep sleep.

In the middle of the night, I woke up. It was quiet. I felt something jump on the end of my bed, and I froze. Whatever was on my bed started walking around my feet. Four feet walking around my feet. I didn't move. I felt the weight. I knew this weight. I knew these movements. I recognized them. My heart began to pound. Oh, my God, he's back! And he was lying on my leg, vibrating warmth and love through my duvet into my body. I couldn't speak. I felt love. I felt coziness. I didn't feel alone. The phone rang, but I was scared to move. Scared it would frighten Cleo away. I answered.

"I got your cat."

I was about to say, "Thanks, but my cat is back,"

when I turned on the lights only to see nothing on my bed but my clothes from the day before. I couldn't believe it. I could have sworn I felt Cleo. I FELT HIM! He was there! I got scared for a moment thinking that maybe he had died and was saying good-bye through astral projection. No. I knew in my heart that Cleo was still alive. I knew it. I knew it, I knew it, I knew it.

"I'll be right over."

I took down the address, jumped back into my clothes on the bed, and got in the car.

A man answered the door. A wiry dude with greasy hair who reminded me of this dealer in the Valley when I was growing up. We exchanged quick hellos and then got down to business.

"Here's your cat."

He shoved this scrawny black kitten toward me. He was about three months old. Definitely not Cleo.

"I'm sorry, but that's not my cat."

"Yes, it is. I'd like my thousand bucks."

An anorexic-looking peroxide-dyed cliché of a broken woman joined him at the door.

"Why the fuck you outta bed! Go back to bed."

"Baby, what are you doing?"

"GO BACK TO YOUR BED!"

"Who's she?"

"I'M GOING TO FUCKING KILL YOU IF YOU DON'T GET BACK INTO BED RIGHT THIS SEC-OND!"

"I should go."

"Whoa whoa whoa. Wait. You owe me money. I've been dealing with this fucking cat!"

"Baabbyyyy."

He twisted the woman's arm and shoved her back inside.

"SHUT UP!"

The woman squeaked out a whimpering cry, and I felt my stomach tensing up and my fists clenching and I wanted to hurt this man. This bully. This liar. This scumbag.

"Now see what you've done? Give me my fucking money, take this stupid cat, and get the fuck out of here before I call the cops."

Was this guy kidding me? I should have been the one calling the cops, or a shelter for battered and abused women to report this pathetic guy. I backed up, scared that he might try to hurt me. I wasn't sure what to do. So I said something like, *"You leave her alone, or else I'll report you."* Kind of lame, but I was scared. I got into my car and drove away.

What a dick. I was worried about the woman.

About the kitty. About what I should do. What I should do about this bully. I really hate bullies. They make me full of rage. I always wonder what kind of child-hood they had to make them so mean-spirited and full of fear. It's been my experience that when you're picked on at home, you will act out in the world. I flashed on this other dickhead that I had long forgotten about.

Kitty Recon

I don't remember his name, but I do remember that he was an asshole. Some dude who my mother hired to do some construction work and painting around the house who always smelled like stale cigarettes and moldy cheese, had a bad attitude, and was always very rude.

I know my father didn't really like him much either. Once he asked my dad if he could keep his six-pack in the fridge. My dad said no, he'd rather him drink after work and not on the job. Duh. But being the brain trust that this guy was, the dickhead put his beer in the freezer, and it totally exploded all over the place. What a genius.

He was one of those guys who is not aware of

anything except for what is directly in front of his nose. Insensitive and bullish, I could not understand why my mother would employ such a brute. And then I found out that apparently he had recommended her for a few interior decorator jobs, so she felt like she owed him.

Right before he started working for us, my parents had gone to Spain and brought me back a little Spanish village made out of ceramic that I would play with for hours. The people were no bigger than two inches high and were very skillfully painted in earth tones with little pops of color. I was around six at the time. The village consisted of the flamenco dancer in her red dress, the handsome matador in his smart little cap and cape, the evil couple dressed in blue, the fat baker and his jolly wife, the farmer and his three mules, and the stuffy banker who didn't seem to have any friends. The village was a regular Peyton Place.

The main story went something like this. The lady in red and the matador were madly in love with each other. The lady in blue, the half sister of the lady in red, was jealous, however, because she, too, was secretly in love with the matador. She made a plot with her husband (the man in blue) to kidnap the lady in red. The man in blue didn't have any problem taking the lady in red away, for he, too, was in love with her. The lady in blue would go to the matador to break the news, crying, pretending to be sad, in the hopes of winning the matador's heart. The whole village would mourn the lady in red's disappearance. She was the dancer of the village and beloved by all. At some point, the man in blue felt guilty and would lead the matador to his love, who was now tied to a tree, and he would save her. Supposedly, the men from the village would go visit the lady in red at night and try to remove her clothes. Even though I was the one making this story up, the implications went right over my head. The lady in blue would be cast aside and thrown out of the village. The story was so clear in my head, it seemed to be telling itself.

My obsession with matadors and flamenco dancers apparently started when I was two and my parents took me to Olvera Street in downtown Los Angeles. At some point they lost me.

"Do you have Gigi?" asked my mother.

"I thought you had her," responded my father.

"Where's Gigi?!" That sort of thing, then total panic. They frantically searched all over, through the taco stands, the mariachi hat store, the piñata stall, until they heard laughing and applause. They went over to see what was going on, only to find their little girl, diapers and all, up on a platform, arms raised and legs stomping, attempting to mimic the flamenco dancers performing onstage. So when I got the Spanish village with the matadors and ladies in red and blue I was ecstatic. I felt like I had been reunited with my people.

So anyway. This bully of a man destroyed my entire Spanish village with his dirty old boot and didn't even bat an eye. Clearly he lacked the sensitivity gene or was a total psychopath. He just walked through my village, crushing the giant snail who on this particular day was threatening the good people of the land. (I would change up the story every now and then, add new villains for the people to bond together over and fight against. Besides the lady in blue and the giant snail, a caterpillar, an "alien leaf person," or a baby lizard sometimes guest starred as the bad guy. I was really into the little people fighting for their freedom and rights against the big, bad world. Good versus Evil 101. It was very satisfying for the good to triumph over and over again in my little universe.

In that day's episode, a gigantic killer snail was slugging his way through the town square. He had already suffocated the baker's wife and was leaving a gnarly trail of goo behind, which the donkeys were getting stuck in—à la the dinosaurs at the La Brea Tar Pits, who got stuck in the tar and died a slow, sinking death. The banker had slipped in the sebaceous slop and broken his hip. Chaos ensued. The townspeople were plotting to pour a barrel of salt onto the monster, when all of a sudden an even bigger giant walked through and crushed the snail!

This was not a heroic act, however. It was the thoughtless gesture of a mindless ogre. The beer-drinking bastard was no doubt on his way to smoke cigarettes while pretending to fix something. He kind of reminded me of the sadistic Leroy from the old film *The Bad Seed.* It was a childhood favorite of mine, which may have accounted for months of detention at school followed by more months of being grounded. He would torment little Rhoda to the point where she had to set his bed on fire. With him in it. Burnt him to a crisp. I always admired that little girl's ingenuity. He was a big bastard as well, and was clearly asking for it. Once again the little people had to fight the big bully. Sure, Rhoda was actually a sociopath, but she was basically my age, so I related to her.

So this brutish man walked right through my

Our cat Spotty and me at my fifth birthday party. To the left was my friend Richi. We would dig for worms and eat dirt together. It was surprisingly tasty.

Spanish village and crushed and killed the snail, leaving him smushed and smeared in the middle of the cement, in the middle of my village.

But that wasn't the worst of it. A short time later my sister's cat, Spotty, a female calico who was very prissy and never my favorite, got into a bit of a jam. Spotty was a drooler. A serious drooler. It was disgusting to me how much she drooled. You would pet her and there would be an instant drool puddle below her chin, dripping onto whatever was below. She was my sister's cat and so I never really got to totally love her. But we tolerated each other's presence. I thought she was a user and highly manipulative, and I didn't buy into her bullshit. She reminded me of one of those Park Avenue gold-digger girls who would marry someone just for money. She wasn't about love. She wanted quilts and tuna and to be pampered all day long. A taker. Never that considerate of anyone around her unless they had something to offer. But still, my sister loved her, so I was respectful.

Apparently Spotty was also a slut. She came home knocked up one day and we had no idea who the father was. She had six kittens. They were so small and helpless. My mother said we could not keep them. We would take them down to the store to give them away once they got a bit older. There were four calico kitties, one solid orange kitten, and a mostly black cat. It made me wonder if there were two fathers. *Was that even possible?* my young brain wondered.

So one day when the asshole was at our house, building a bar in the family room, I was playing outside, and out of nowhere I heard a very faint, squeaky sound. I couldn't figure out what it was or where it was coming from, so I started to investigate.

The noise got louder as I wandered toward the side of the house where the dickhead's stuff was all gathered. Suddenly I noticed one of his canvas sacks was moving. As I got closer I realized that the squeaky sounds were actually little mews that the kittens would make. Holy crap! Inside a knotted canvas bag were all of the kittens! He was obviously taking them away! A kitten-napping, as it were. They were all piled on top of one another, scared and trying to escape. I can't imagine what this sadistic maniac had planned, but thoughts of him throwing the poor, innocent kitties into the sea came to mind. Spotty came running over and began to paw at the bag, pleading with me to help save her babies. I had to act fast. I didn't know when the asshole was going to show up and cart the kitties away. The sense of injustice infuriated me, but I would deal with the bad man and my mother later (assuming she knew what was going on).

I couldn't untie the knots that held the bag together! He was obviously a seasoned cat-napper and knew how to tie a professional knot. I ran into the kitchen and grabbed a pair of enormous scissors and a box. As soon as I got outside, I went to work on the bag. I carefully cut a hole big enough to rescue the kitties. I put them in the box and took them to the closet in the playroom. I gave them a bowl of milk to keep them happy and quiet, just until their abductor went away and my sister got home.

Later that day, when my mother finally came back, I told her what had happened and asked how she could have let such a cruel thing take place. I was crying and outraged and demanding answers. She was just as upset as I was and couldn't believe her builder could have done such a thing. As it turned out, he had said he was going to help her find homes for the kittens, but his method of transportation shocked and upset my mother as much as it did me. She ended up firing him, thank God, and my sister and I took the kittens down to Thrifty's and found them all nice people to give them a home.

I felt a sense of pride that I had never experienced before. I had saved the innocent and helpless and had gotten rid of the bad guy, all in one afternoon. It had been a very fulfilling, super fantastic day.

CHAPTER TEN

The Dream

ONE UNMOTIVATED MORNING I SETTLED into a relatively new routine—namely, watching one of those evangelists on TV. This had become a habit of mine, along with listening to them on the radio. Even when I was young I always loved the feeling of going into church. I loved the smell of frankincense. I loved the gospel choirs. I loved the cross necklaces. It's not that I was particularly religious; I just enjoyed the theatrics that the church had to offer. They were believers! And these shows were great! Laughter! Praise! Tears! Miracles! It's not that I'm against other religions;

it's just that I couldn't find any good programs on TV promoting them in such an uplifting, entertaining way! I couldn't believe how much makeup and hairspray all these Christians used. Was that just for TV, or did they walk around that way all the time? It reminded me of the old country music saying, "The higher the hair, the closer to God." Is this where they got it from? Does that apply to mascara as well? "The thicker the lash, the more one can see the divine"? Maybe I could glean some sort of hopeful message that would renew my faith and get me through the day. Maybe my prayers were being overshadowed by my cynicism. Maybe I needed to eat something. I hadn't gone shopping for food since I don't know when. I decided that a good meal would clear my head, so I drove down to one of my breakfast joints in West Hollywood. The lot was packed, so I parked up the street and began to walk down a block crowded with stores that were chock-full of consumer goods that no one really needed. The trashy lingerie store where they display prepubescent female mannequins in hookerwear right in the window for everyone to see. The 99 cent store—a place for crap. And my personal favorite: a store full of gefilte fish, menorahs, and mezuzahs half price all year long—it might as well have been called Jews "R" Us. Next thing I knew, a dark old gypsy woman was banging on her window, beckoning me to come inside her shop. I politely shook my head, but she was insistent, her pounding urgent, like she needed to tell me something. I had time to kill, so I figured what the fuck.

I sat down. She took my hand into hers. It was tattooed and had at least eleven rings on it, and the dirt underneath her nails seemed to have been there for decades.

Long life. *Blah blah blah*, artistic, *blah blah blah*, bullshit, *blah blah blah*, whatever, *blah blah blah*. You've lost something dear to you.

Bingo!

"Yes! As a matter of fact, yes!"

In a fast and high voice, I told her about my cat and appreciated the fact that she didn't lie and tell me where to find him but instead brought out a little sculpture of some lady. It was Saint Gertrude, the patron saint and protector of cats everywhere.

"You should have this," she told me.

"How much?"

"A gift."

"Wow, thanks."

She kissed my forehead and blessed me.

I turned to leave.

The gypsy lady who gave me my St. Gertrude statue

"Has the matador found you?"

This stopped me in my tracks. I slowly turned back around to face her.

"What do you mean?"

"Has the cycle been broken?"

"I don't know what you are talking about." And at the time I was so obsessed with Cleo that I really didn't know what she was talking about.

She smiled mysteriously and disappeared behind a curtain into the back.

I left. It wasn't until after I'd eaten my breakfast and was driving back home that it hit me. Shit! The dream. The *dream.* I flashed back to the dream.

It always starts the same.

I'm around thirty years old, and I'm wearing an old and tattered red Spanish dancer's dress. It's strange to be three in real life and to see myself as a grown-up. I've just finished my shift after a long night and am hanging up my dancing shoes, which are tied together, on a rusty nail sticking out of an old wooden wall. I'm tired. I feel heavy. And sad. And lonely. And I'm in a bar. The bar is rundown with decrepit types, their drunken heads passed out on the dirty bar counter. There are only a few people left. I slowly walk through the saloon-style wooden doors and find myself on an old dusty road with no particular place to go. Dawn is breaking. A quiet bass line begins to play and my body tenses up. I feel scared all of a sudden. I look back down the road, and in the distance I see the black Cadillac, cruising up the street like a panther stalking its prey. I know it is coming to get me. I begin to speed up in order to get away from the car. My heart begins to beat faster, as does the music. Bada dum de dum da de dum. Bada dum de dum da de dum . . .

At this point, I'm running and scared shitless and the car is gaining on me. I see just an arm, dressed in black, come out of the window, pointing a gun at me. I know that this belongs to my jealous boyfriend, the matador. He shoots me in my left upper back, right under my shoulder. I scream and wake up in a panic.

It's always the same dream. It started when I was around three years old. I can't emphasize enough how odd it was to see myself as a grown-up, knowing without a doubt that the thirty-year-old dancer was *me*. Even then, I'd wake up in a panic, not really understanding but knowing that what happened felt *very* real.

Was that why I was so obsessed with the little Spanish village story? Is that why I instinctually went to dance with the flamenco dancers at Olvera Street? Was this a past-life thing? As I mentioned earlier on, when

I first met my boyfriend (the one who I broke up with at the beginning of this tale) there was a strange feeling of recognition. As though we knew each other. But the thing that really caught my attention was when I went over to his house for the first time, he had paintings of matadors EVERYWHERE. I asked him what was up with that. He just shrugged and told me he had always had this strange obsession with them for no particular reason. Another random coincidence. And I always sensed that his ex-girlfriend, with whom I had become very close, was still secretly in love with him and would have liked to get me gone. Consequently, her mother and I became very close as well, and we used to joke that she was really *my* mother. And they happened to be of Spanish descent! It was as though the lady in blue was the ex-girlfriend/sister and I was the lady in red. Of course the ex was the matador. The dynamics were all the same. All very strange.

So who knows, maybe my ex *was* the matador from my dream. Maybe that was my past life. Maybe the gypsy lady knew a little bit more than she was letting on . . . or not. Maybe I was just losing it. A rational person would roll her eyes and tell me it was time to go back to work.

But I must admit, I don't talk about this often, but since we are on the subject of past lives, I will tell you.

My Spanish dancer look. Olé.

You have read this far. I feel much closer to you and sense that I can tell you anything.

Past-life Husband

I've never believed in one-night stands. I tend to be more of a relationship girl—a serial monogamist, if you will. The idea of letting some stranger have his way with you and then just leave—no romance, no love—makes me feel anxious and angry. Who wants to be left behind after a night of passionate lovemaking? If I had sex with a stranger, and then he were to just walk away, I would feel so enraged that I would just want to kill him. I totally get the whole praying mantis/black widow syndrome where the female eats the male after mating with him. The instinct being, "I will fuck you, but then I will kill you." Easy, clean, concise.

Some theories try to make the male praying mantises and black widows martyrs instead of victims.

"Oh, they sacrifice themselves to the female so she gets the proper nourishment for their offspring." Blah blah blah . . . I don't buy it. That certainly wouldn't happen with the males of the human species. I think they are probably just so dumbstruck after sex that they would realize too late, "Oh, shit! My arms and half my back are gone. Oh, no!" Poor dumb bastards. My theory? You fuck me and then fuck me over, you fucking insect, you will die. No spreading your seed to other bitches. No turning into an asshole. The mother could simply say to her offspring, "Your father was a very devoted, attentive man. Then he sacrificed his life for you. Now he is dead." But I digress.

What about the times, you may ask, that you are just so horny that you just gotta have it? What's a girl to do? Well, that's where my fantasy invention, the Sex Lobotomy Machine, might come in handy. Because, sure, we all have the fantasy of having sex with some random person every now and then, but the reality of it is just too brutal. Think *Men in Black* memory zapper. Same concept. What if we could have our way with whomever we choose, and then just zap 'em so they don't remember a thing? Shit, if it wasn't any good— or even worse, if you find yourself getting emotionally attached to some vapid ogre—zap that memory away immediately! Just think of the convenience for these women who want to get pregnant without the fuss and mess of a male partner. Seduce 'em, fuck 'em, then zap 'em! No one's the wiser when that baby is born, and it's all yours without another annoying opinion in sight.

Unfortunately, as I said, this is just a fantasy, so in reality I just avoid one-night stands. Please. Let me move on to the story I was going to tell you.

Several years ago, I was filming—and I use the term loosely—this "movie" in the Philippines, when I decided to escape for one night and fly to Hong Kong for a little respite from the insanity on the set. I was only in Hong Kong for one night, and while standing on the sidewalk waiting for the sheets of rain to sub-side, suddenly my insides were pulled so hard by some force that I had to turn around, only to see a tall man accompanied by three women going downstairs to an underground walkway. Strange, I thought. When he resurfaced two minutes later, across the street, every instinct in me told me to follow him. By the time he entered a bar called the Malibu Café a few blocks away (ironic, me being a California girl and all), I felt like I knew everything about this man, even without speak-ing to him. And even though I never got a clear look at his face, I *knew* that he was European. I knew his age. I just *knew* that he was a designer of some sort.

So I followed him into the bar. I went right up to him and struck up a conversation. The three ladies he walked in with were clearly talking to other people and not a deterrent at all. As it turned out, he was from

Antwerp, where, incidentally, my grandfather was born, but now lived in Amsterdam. He was forty years old, as suspected, and he was a menswear designer. And even after he told me his name, I had the strangest urge to call him something else. A different man's name. We talked for a while, danced for a bit, started kissing, and eventually went back to his hotel. This was something I wouldn't normally do, but it felt as though we had known each other forever and that this was inevitable.

Later that night, I experienced flashes of another time. I saw this warm, cozy home with a beautiful hearth and food cooking and a few kids running around. I could smell it. I could feel it. I felt calm and content and safe, and I absolutely knew without a doubt that this guy was my husband in a past life. It's hard to explain, but I just knew. I didn't say a word to him about it, but then he, in a very confused state, said to me, "I know this sounds crazy, but I feel like you are or were my wife from a different time. I don't even believe in that kind of thing but . . ."

Not to get into too many details (this is not a book for anyone to whack off to, and besides, it's much sexier if you make it up in your head), but it was one of the most intense nights of my life. When I had to leave in the morning, we were crying and promising each other that we would be together no matter what. It was so difficult to leave. He wrote to me that he told his wife everything. (Oh, did I forget to mention that he had a wife?!) Well, I didn't know about the Mrs. until the wee hours of the morning when he confessed that he had never cheated on her in ten years and how strange this whole thing was. Due to the utterly confused look on his face, I believed him. He wasn't trying to hide the fact that he had a wedding ring on, but me, being a stupid American, didn't realize that Europeans wore their marriage vows on their *right* hand instead of the left. After that he kept sending me letters saying that every day he was trying to think of ways for us to be together. And every day I grew more and more skeptical about how this could really work.

He asked me to please come to their home in Amsterdam, that his wife *really* wanted to meet me. The Dutch. Go figure. I did want a partner, but not a married one, no matter how "Dutch" his wife was. I sadly let him go.

And so who knows—my ex very well *could* have been the matador from my dream, and the matador *could* have been a lover from a past life. And who knows—this guy could have *really* been my husband from another lifetime. Some things just can't be explained in a scientific way.

CHAPTER ELEVEN

One Foot In, One Foot Out of Heaven

ONE DAY THE MOST OBVIOUS solution for how to find Cleo hit me. It was as simple as flying to New York and going to my dentist. Why hadn't I thought of this before? Please, indulge me while I explain. . . .

Through the years I had experienced some gnarly times at the dentist. The most uncomfortable being once when I went to get my teeth cleaned in Los Angeles. I was living a bicoastal life, so I needed two dentists, one in L.A. and one in New York. My trusted L.A. hygienist was on vacation and there was a substitute in her place. With a smile on her face and weapons in her hands, she told me to open wide and relax. There seemed to be something odd about her, but I thought I was just being paranoid. You should always listen to your instincts.

As soon as her instruments of torture were scraping my very sensitive gums, she cheerfully told me that she wasn't really a hygienist but in fact a journalist. Oh, sure, she went to dental school, but her true passion was writing about movies. One of her favorite movies of all time was *Bound*, where I played a lesbian who had just gotten out of jail and got involved with Jennifer Tilly's character in a major scam and fell in love with her along the way. My whole body began to tense up as she told me how she had given me a great review, how the movie changed her life, and how she and her friends were all wondering, "Are you gay?" This chick had very sharp tools inside my very vulnerable mouth, and I immediately flashed to the famous scene in *Marathon Man* where Laurence Olivier's character, a Nazi dentist, asks Dustin Hoffman's clueless character, "Is it safe?" before plunging the sharp tool into Hoffman's gums. Oh, my God.

I kept trying to catch the receptionist's eye with a hand signal of help, but she wasn't paying attention. What was I to do? How should I reply to escape this situation, gums and teeth intact??

"Are you gay?" she sinisterly repeated.

Trying to protect myself from bodily harm, I gave her the answer I thought she wanted to hear. *"Oh, yes. I'm gay. Super-duper gay. As gay as it gets! Gay, gay, gay!!!"*

"Really?"

"Uh, no . . . not gay at all!! Incredibly straight! As straight as an arrow! Unbelievably straight!"

By this time I was sweating profusely, and she started to tell me how she was also really into astrology and played the stock market as well, and how she could read my chart and help me make money and blah blah blah. Help! Get me the fuck out of here!

I told the dental office about her later and how to NEVER let her do my teeth again. They said they were so sorry and had let her go anyway. But she had somehow gotten my number (looked through my files, no doubt) and began stalking me. Good times. Good times.

Needless to say, I'm a bit scared of new people working on my teeth.

So when I had a cavity, I went to my New York

guy. I sat down in the friendly family dentist's chair and he very pleasantly asked me if I would like some gas before he started. Nitrous oxide, otherwise known as laughing gas, gives one an exhilarated feeling while operating as an anesthetic. I had never had it before, but I'm always open to new, chemically induced experiences, so I said sure.

He placed the mask around my nose, and after about a minute or two of inhaling this sweetly odored vapor, I started feeling light-headed and very relaxed. I became super-aware of every sound around me. The drill became the bass, the clinking of tools the high hat, the murmuring of voices the melody, and the honking cars and buses from outside turned into very cool drum sounds. This shit was great! I had a whole orchestra playing in my head, and then, as has happened when I've done other hallucinatory drugs, I began to choreograph a lovely ballet in my head. Everything was a pleasant hue of orange as the dancers performed across the "stage." I was really enjoying myself, completely forgetting about the barbaric acts that were occurring in my mouth. Then, suddenly out of nowhere, a very distinct man's voice boomed, "Leave your boyfriend. He is not good enough for you." (He kind

of sounded like a white version of James Earl Jones's
Darth Vader.) This really interrupted my reverie. I
blinked my eyes open and looked at the dentist. With
my mouth full off appliances, I asked him very pointedly, *"What?"*

"I didn't say anything. Are you okay? Should I
turn down the gas?"

"No, I'm fine," I lied. I was a little freaked out but
curious enough to go back to my orange daze and hear
some more words from the man in the ethers.

He proceeded to tell me how my boyfriend at the
time had been cheating on me, and with whom, and
I needed to break up with him. He said this all in a
very matter-of-fact, nonjudgmental way. This seemed
strange to me, since I was pretty into my boyfriend at
the time and had no clue about any of this. A few
months later, however, the truth came out. The liar
had been totally cheating on me with all of the people
the voice told me about. He was a total dick about it,
and I felt hurt and betrayed. This was definitely not
unconditional love. I broke up with him immediately
and realized just how toxic the relationship had become.
It was like an emotional crash diet. I felt as light as a
feather. Whoa. How did this guy know this stuff? Was

he the inner wizard in my head, or was he seriously like the voice of God. Or perhaps one of God's assistants?

I thought it was just one of those things and didn't obsess on it too much, until I had to go back to the dentist to replace a few cavities with porcelain and remove the archaic mercury fillings.

Once again he offered me gas. I politely accepted. The orchestra began to play. The lighting began to reflect a heavenly orange hue. The dancers began to pirouette, and then suddenly the voice was back.

"A relationship is like a tooth."

He then proceeded to give a lecture about the foundation of the relationship, how if there is a cavity that is not replaced, it will soon rot and you will lose the whole tooth, and perhaps even part of the jaw, etc. It all made perfect sense. A brilliant analogy summing up what makes a healthy relationship (or tooth). This guy was kind of a genius. I wondered how if a cavity is like a bad boyfriend, what did that make plaque? Perhaps plaque was when one person has a really annoying habit, and you ask them to please be aware of it in order to keep the relationship healthy? Unless they are diligent, they will keep doing the annoying habit, and then the plaque has the potential to turn into a cavity. What about flossing? Is that equivalent to going to your boyfriend's parents' house for dinner, even though you can't stand them? Crest whitening strips clearly would be couples therapy, no?

So now I've had two nitrous oxide–induced episodes involving an omniscient, disembodied Wizard of Oz–like voice who shares his wisdom with me in the dental chair. There's no place like home. There's no place like home. Obviously, I had to book a dental appointment to speak to the Wizard and ask him where I could find my beloved Cleo.

It wasn't time for a cleaning, but I called my new and improved L.A. dental office and told them that something was bothering me and I should come in. As it turns out, I really did need a root canal. (Oh, the powers of the mind.) Bummed about the root canal, but excited about the gas, I went in. The dentist said it may hurt a bit, so he would give me extra gas. Who was I to disagree? Extra gas, extra wisdom?

As the orchestra started to play, and everything began to take on an orange hue, I very respectfully asked the voice to please tell me where I could find my cat. The dancers began their intoxicated ballet. But there was no voice. The second act began. This time, a weird serpentlike character showed up and the dance became more Pina Bausch–like, with the dancers hopping to and fro, avoiding the monster. One of them kept yelling for pizza. It was getting weird, but still no voice. Shit. Maybe he was mad at me for making a request. Maybe it didn't work that way. Maybe I'd just had too much gas! Then out of nowhere, sounding very far away, the voice very calmly appeared.

"One foot in, one foot out of heaven."

Period. Silence. Nothing.

Usually the voice was right above me, slightly to the right, but this time he was far away.

What?

He repeated it: "One foot in, one foot out of heaven."

What the fuck does that mean? I need more! I am in a lot of pain and I need answers! Somehow I realized that if I wanted to know what he was talking about, I had to go to where he was. Somewhere outside and beyond the dentist's office. I wanted to know so badly what he was talking about that my desire and will transported me. I saw the clichéd version of the aerial view of me in the dentist's chair. Next thing I knew, I was in a very twilight-dark, gray atmosphere, full of hazy lights shooting around like headlights on a foggy night. In fact, *we* were light sources as well. No one had bodies. The voice and I were in a deep discussion. He was providing me answers to the really big cosmic questions. Why are we here? What is the purpose of life? How did the universe really begin? Who makes the best pastrami sandwich in NYC? I don't know if I was having a near-death experience or a serious hallucination or what.

Either way, at this point I didn't give a shit about my relationships anymore. My career didn't mean a thing. I didn't have any attachment to my family or friends. I didn't even really care about finding Cleo! It all seemed so small compared to how expansive I felt, and next to the really important matters at hand, my life on earth seemed trivial. Wow! Why couldn't I feel like that all of the time?! It was amazing! Then I realized, *One foot in, one foot out of heaven.* That must be the in-between zone. Not quite on earth, not quite the next stop. Maybe it's the place where the crazy people live. I've heard about how in some cultures people revere the crazy ones because they think that they are closer to God. Wherever I was, I liked it. I was freer, more knowledgeable, and felt incredibly content.

I'm not even sure that I wanted to go back. Was I ready to totally abandon my former life and live there? Did I even know how to get back? Did I really want to deal with the pain of the aftermath of a root canal? The moment fear started to rear its reasonable head, I shot back into my body. I could feel my mouth again. I was back in the dentist's chair. Whoa. That was really a trip.

Unfortunately, the voice hadn't revealed anything about the whereabouts of Cleo, but I did discover that I wasn't afraid of death anymore. My own death, that is. When others die, it still sucks. But if this place was any indication as to what happens when we die, then I don't have as much anxiety about it. It was a pretty incredible atmosphere. It wasn't quite my time yet, there in the old dentist's chair, but the profound experience certainly gave me a new appreciation for the whole thing.

Back to the real world. My search continued.

CHAPTER TWELVE

Big Blue Diamond in the Sky

IT WAS A BEAUTIFUL L.A. morning. Crisp air, blue skies, and relatively no smog. I forgot my can of tuna and knife on this particular day. After about an hour of no luck, I slumped down onto the sidewalk, discouraged, disheartened, and frankly tired of this whole charade. The phone rang.

"Dahhhling, don't be discouraged. Cleo can hear you calling out to him, he is very close, but he is still too angry to come out. He may need a few more weeks. Now get up and keep your eyes peeled for clues."

It was Sonia. Amazing.

"My eyes peeled? What does that mean?"

"Don't worry, dahhhling . . . just keep looking. You will get help. You will get Cleo back, I promise you."

And like Glinda the Good Witch, floating away on her bubble after a few words of encouragement, Sonia hung up and was gone. Whoa. Weird.

I put the phone back in my pocket with a new-found burst of hope, and then I noticed these two black crows circling overhead. They were making so much noise, cawing at me, until I noticed that they wanted me to follow them. I only knew this because when I stopped and took notice of them, they went to a location and furiously pecked their beaks down on a pole or fence. I walked to the spot, and then they flew to another location. When I stopped following them, they circled my head and started cawing again. I know it sounds crazy (even Arthur was skeptical when I told him that the birds were helping me track down Cleo). I told him how Sonia said that the two spirits were going to help me find Cleo. I had already told Arthur about Uncle Jack and Teddy.

"So you are saying that you think the crows are your Uncle Jack and Teddy?"

"I know it sounds insane, Arthur, but stranger things have happened. Well, maybe not, but you never know."

He looked at me with concern and pity.

"We gonna find your kitty, sugar."

I know it sounds crazy. I know that animals don't talk to people. Although, I did have a weird experience with Kalookie when I was, like, ten. But at this point I could tell Arthur anything and I knew he would never judge me. He understood me more than most. So I went ahead and told him the story.

Kalookie and I slept together every night. My bed was right under a large window, and although it had bars on it (to keep the burglars out or me in?), I could still see the silhouette of the trees and the stars in the sky. One night a voice woke me from my sleep. "Get up! You've got to wake up! You've gotta check this out!" The voice was that of a young man. Eager, urgent, and with the tone of a tenor. Much to my surprise, the voice belonged to Kalookie! (Huh. I always figured Kalookie would have a much lower voice if he could speak.) He kept nudging me until I looked out the window to where he was staring. I thought I must have been dreaming, of course—I didn't really think that Kalookie could actually talk—but when I sat up to make sure I was awake, I looked out my window, and I saw the craziest, brightest, bluest star in the sky, right between the two bars. It literally looked like a big blue diamond. I rubbed my eyes again, but the huge, blue star remained.

"Isn't that amazing?" Kalookie asked. We both stared in silence, and after a few moments he asked me if he could go outside because there was this really cute new cat down the street and he wanted to go meet her. I never let him out before it was light for fear of coyotes, but he kept pleading with me, promising he'd be careful, until finally I said, *"Okay."* We jumped out of bed together, and I let him out the back door, making him promise to be home before I went to school in the morning. He said thanks and took off into the night.

When I woke up in the morning and saw Kalookie asleep next to my head, I figured I must have dreamt the whole thing. But it felt so real. Especially since I had "woken up" to sit up and gaze out the window in the night. Then I noticed there were muddy kitty paw prints on my bed that hadn't been there the night before. Kalookie was fast asleep with what looked like a smile on his face. When I got up to go to breakfast, Marie was grumbling that "that nasty cat had gotten out somehow" and had raced in when she had opened the back door early this morning. She was "gonna whoop his ass."

Arthur didn't say a word. He just listened and slightly nodded his head.

I then noticed that the circling birds were back. I pointed upward, and when Arthur saw them he said with wonder, "I ain't never seen nothing like that before." They indeed eventually led me to a dark gray cat underneath a bush. Unfortunately, it wasn't Cleo. But I thanked the crows for trying and continued on my way. Sonia. Wow. I guess she really knew her shit.

· CHAPTER THIRTEEN ·

John from Jail

I WAS ON THE PHONE WITH my ex, el matador, try-ing to be normal, when all of a sudden I got a call-waiting beep and switched over. Instead of a human voice, I heard a recorded message:

"Hello, this is the county jail with a collect call from *John*. Do you accept the charges?"

Obviously it was the wrong number. I replied no and switched back to my other conversation, and then the phone beeped again.

"Hello, this is the county jail with a collect call

from *I know how to find your cat!* Do you accept the charges?"

"OH, MY GOD! YES!"

I click over. I tell my ex I gotta go. Some guy from jail is calling and he knows where Cleo is. I click back over.

"HELLO?" Dial tone. Shit. Fuck. I hung up on the one guy who knows where Cleo is. I started panicking. The phone rang again.

"Hello, this is the county jail with a call from *Don't hang up.* Do you accept the charges?"

"YES, YES, YES!"

Then all of a sudden, a man's voice, maybe mid-thirties, frantically said, "Hey, don't put me on hold. It'll disconnect."

"Don't worry, I won't. I got it."

"Hi. Thanks for picking up."

"Sure, where's my cat?"

"Well, I read about it in the classified ads," he said, and then he paused. "This is what's going on. My name is John and I got busted with a DUI and I've been in a jail for about three hours now. My wife doesn't know where I am and I want to call her but we have a special block on her phone and she won't know it's me. So if you can help me call her, she will get me out and we will help you find your cat. We are cat people, too. I can only imagine what you are going through."

Something seemed strange about this. But he seemed so sympathetic, his voice so friendly and soothing, and well, let's face it, I was desperate.

"Um, okay."

"Great. Now this is what you do."

He instructed me on the art of the three-way call from jail.

"Now, it is really important that I blow into the phone as you dial. So they don't hear you dialing and disconnect the call."

I was thinking, *Boy, John's learned a lot in his short time in the slammer.* But I dialed, he blew, it rang. I whispered, *"Okay, John, you can stop blowing."* He stopped. All of a sudden a trailer-trash voice answers the phone.

"Hello?"

"Charlene?"

"Yeah?"

"It's John!"

"I know who it is! Why the FUCK are you calling me? I never want to hear from your sorry ass ever again! You are NOT ALLOWED to call me! I'm gonna get the police on you, John. AGAIN!"

"Baby."

"Don't you 'baby' me, you fucking asshole." She slammed the phone down. There was a beat of silence.

"That didn't go so well, John."

"No, it did not." I felt kinda hurt at this moment.

"You lied to me, John. That wasn't your wife."

"I know. I'm sorry. That was my girlfriend."

"Doesn't sound like she's your girlfriend anymore, John."

"I know."

"I gotta go."

"But no, wait. I can still help you find your cat."

"How, John? How are you gonna help me find my cat? You're in jail."

"I know. But maybe if you help me get out . . ."

I cut him off. *"No, no, no, no, no. Good-bye, John."*

"Wait, please. You sound really beautiful."

I slammed down the phone. Another dream shattered.

· CHAPTER FOURTEEN ·

Stalker Kitty

WHEN I WAS GROWING UP, my mom always warned me never to talk to strangers. This advice proved to be sound when one day when I was walking home from school. I was seven, and I was feeling extra jaunty in my new white rabbit-fur coat. Faux, of course (I was only seven, for God's sake). Speaking of which, can you imagine in today's world just letting your seven-year-old walk home by herself? But back then, life in the Valley seemed so innocent and uncomplicated and safe. And it was, right up until that day.

I was in a particularly good mood that Tuesday afternoon. I decided to stop by the Kleins' house to get something to eat. It was more or less expected. My brother and Alan Klein were best friends and are to this day. My mother and father traveled a great deal, so Dann started to eat at Alan's house, and eventually my sister and I joined him. We would raid their kitchen on a daily basis. I used to walk the long way home so I could stop by their house for an after-school snack, which inevitably turned into dinner. Unlike our house, the Kleins' cupboard was always freshly stocked with the necessities of life. Ding Dongs, Chips Ahoy! cookies, Twinkies, Sno Balls, Hot Tamales, and pretty much anything else that was sweet and nourishing. They even had a separate refrigerator in the garage filled with every type of soda pop known to mankind. You name it, they had it. It was sugar junkie heaven and just what the doctor (probably not my dentist) ordered after a tough day in first grade. So whether anyone was there or not, I would let myself in and make myself at home. For that matter, so did my whole family. You could say it was a home away from home, only this one was stocked with food.

Sometimes I would bring a friend, make a party out of it. But on this day, I was alone. And when I was leaving the Kleins' after my successful gorge, a powder-blue Chevy Malibu pulled up alongside me, just as I was passing the Danger Trees—these huge eucalyptus trees that, in my mind, spelled out the word *danger* in their branches. So this car pulled up. Actually, it slightly cut off my path, so I had no choice, despite my mother's advice, but to answer the driver when he asked me, "Hey, do you know where Collins School is?"

When I decided to be helpful and give the stranger directions, I looked in the window of the car and realized that he didn't have any clothes on. I didn't want to be rude and stare, but there was this THING sticking straight up between his legs. I'd never seen anything like that before, and I couldn't help but wonder, *How could it do that?*

I averted my eyes and efficiently answered, "Well, I know where Collins *Street* is, or Collier Street *School* is, but I don't know of a Collins School. . . ." The stranger then charmingly insisted that the next time he saw me he was going to shove that "thing" up my ass. And he quickly drove away. Talk about rude.

I was a little shocked and not really sure what had just happened. I began to get scared and run home, and then I noticed that the car was behind me now, cruising down the street again, like a great white shark. I very swiftly walked up to some strange house, pretended it was mine, and just walked right in. I was lucky that the door was open and that there wasn't an attack dog. The car passed, and then I ran like hell the rest of the way home, safely into Marie's knees as she opened up the front door.

She asked me what was wrong, and I told her about the incident and she immediately said, "You've got to tell Mr. Stan."

The last thing I wanted to tell my father was about a naked man saying that nasty thing to me. When you're seven years old, the idea of saying the word *penis* to a grown-up was absolutely horrifying. She marched me into his office, and after I uncomfortably mumbled the story to him, he simply nodded and excused me to go play. I thought that was that and decided to forget about the whole thing. Later that night, my parents called me to come into the living room. When I got there, there were two uniformed policemen with notepads. My parents told me to tell them what had happened. In detail. Looking down at the ground, I simply told them that a man in a car had asked me for directions; then he said something mean and drove away. The cop with the mustache was probing me for extra details.

"What was he wearing?"

"*Uh, nothing.*"

"What exactly did you see?"

"*Uh, you know . . . you know . . .*"

This went back and forth several times: me looking at my parents for help, them telling me to go ahead and tell the cop exactly what I saw, for their records. . . .

Finally, embarrassed, harassed, and fed up, I screamed at the top of my lungs, "*HIS PENIS!*" Then I ran out of the room. My brother and sister thought it was the funniest thing ever, me yelling that word to a cop, and couldn't stop laughing. I was teased about it for weeks. Anyway. The points being these: You don't talk to strangers. You don't get in weird cars with strangers. And one would assume that letting a stranger into your home would fall under the category of a Bozo No-No.

So why, might you ask, would I just let this slightly off, odd cat into my home one Sunday morning when I had just moved to Santa Monica after I had graduated from college? It seemed harmless enough at the time.

I wouldn't say it was love at first sight, but me with my need at the time for people to love me (thank God I've grown out of that tedious syndrome), I was definitely super-nice to the strange orange kitty. I gained his trust, and within an hour he was eating out of my hand. Literally. It's funny how cats seem to really go for Chinese leftovers.

He started to pop up every other day when I would get home. We would hang out, pet each other, play a bit. Then one day I had to leave, and he refused to let me go. He literally blocked the door, and if I tried to get by he would swat at me and bite my knees. I thought it was playful at first, but when his tail became three times its normal size and a low, guttural growl began to emanate from his throat, I started to get a bit concerned. I told him to stop it and shook my purse at him. He moved just enough for me to get out the door, and luckily he ran out after me. *Fuck him*, I thought. He was acting like a petulant dickhead. I didn't need this shit in my life. When I came home later that night, he tried to sneak in behind me, but I blocked his way and shut the door really fast behind me, keeping him outside. I figured he would just go away.

He didn't.

The next day when I was walking up to my front door, I very carefully looked around to make sure the coast was clear before opening it. He was nowhere to be seen. Suddenly, as soon as the door opened, he leapt from behind the bushes and ran past me, right into the house. An ambush! I was pissed. I threw down my bags and tried to chase him outside, but to no avail. He hid, and after I had exhausted myself looking for him, I thought, *Fine, I'll just ignore him.*

I was reading on my couch when I felt him rub against my leg, and he looked up at me all innocent-like. Now he was being nice, so I pet him and he began to lick my hand almost as an apology, but then the kisses began to become a bit more aggressive. Before I knew it, he had his claws in my arm so I couldn't move as he kept kissing me, and the weird noises began again. Then he wrapped his entire body around my arm and began dry-humping me like some horny fifteen-year-old boy. I was appalled. This really was unacceptable behavior, not to mention gross. I threw him off me, which just seemed to excite him more. He began chasing me around the table, looking like some sex-crazed lunatic, fat erect tail and all. I had no choice but to run to the bathroom and lock the door.

This was ridiculous. My phone was out in the living room and I was locked in my own bathroom, afraid of a cat. What would I have done anyway? Call 911 and tell them that some lunatic cat was trying to rape me? They would send some nice men over in clean white coats who would cart me off to the funny farm. No. I had to deal with this on my own. I thought I would address him in a very adult manner, tell him he was being super-uncool, and politely ask him to get the fuck out of my house. Great. I love it when I have a plan. So I quietly snuck out of the bathroom, took a deep breath, walked into the living room, and then stopped dead in my tracks. . . .

Demento was sitting upright on my couch, legs spread, licking his very prominent pink kitty boner. Oh, my God. He looked right at me with this nasty, lascivious look on his face and continued to give himself a kitty-licking blowjob. It completely freaked me out. I grabbed my things and ran out of my apartment.

For the next few weeks, I avoided him like the plague. I asked a few neighbors if they knew this cat, but none of them had ever seen him. So the moral of the story is, don't talk to naked strangers in beat-up powder-blue cars, don't invite demented pervo kitty cats into your home, and definitely don't give guys from jail your home phone number. No good will come of any of it.

CHAPTER FIFTEEN

Letting Go

AFTER TWO UNSUCCESSFUL MONTHS of disappointment and heartbreak, with no more than posers and imposters to show for my efforts, I decided enough was enough. It was time to end my search and try to let Cleo go. I knew in my bones that Cleo was still alive, and hopefully he was somewhere where he was loved and happy. Although, I admit, in my insecure moments, I pictured Cleo being cuddled and kissed by hot girls in bikinis, pouring tuna juice into his mouth, and I was jealous. But I had to take the high road. I hoped that he was happy.

I made the grown-up decision to be at peace with this and move on with my life. I mean, how much more of this could I take? Between the late-night phone calls, Doris the psychic, Santeria man, Sonia the animal psychic, the animal shelters, the crystal man, the light-in-his-mouth Deepak Chopra–wannabe guy, John from jail, germaphobic war vet guy, the gypsy lady, and urinating in bottles—there's only so much a person can take! My life had become insane. I was exhausted. It was time to let go.

A few days after I made this decision, I was taking a hot bath, with all these peaceful thoughts swimming through my head, when the phone rang. A very gruff, no-nonsense voice said, "I think I found your cat." After two hundred of these calls I was not enthusiastic.

"Fine . . . I'll be there in an hour."

I was in no hurry, because I knew that it wasn't going to be Cleo. And frankly, at this point I was sick of being disappointed. I had accepted my fate to be alone, which brought up feelings about my first love, Kalookie, and when I lost him.

Kalookie had not been feeling well. He had started looking glassy-eyed and moving a lot slower and cleaning himself a lot less. At this point, I was around fifteen years old and Kalookie had been in my life for approximately eight years. When we took him to the vet, they told us he had a certain kind of kitty leukemia and that they had to do more tests. I would ride my bike every day to the vet's office and hold Kalookie and tell him it was going to be all right. He had weird tubes coming out of him, and he was getting skinnier by the day. I'd always ride my bike home, tears streaming down my face, convincing myself that he would be okay.

One night after my "modeling" job, where I would sit for this artist to sketch my portrait, I walked into the house, only to find my parents waiting in the hallway. I could immediately sense that something was off. My dad was a big man, but somehow he looked as though he wanted to shrink into oblivion; he was leaning against the archway, looking at the floor, unable to look me in the eye.

"What?"

My mother and father didn't know how to tell me that they had decided to put Kalookie to sleep. My breath started to get short, and the floor became wobbly underneath my feet. They told me that he was suffering and that putting him to sleep was the best thing we could do for him. They continued to explain, but I didn't hear a thing. The pounding in my ears obliterated any words that were coming out of their mouths. I started crying and screaming all at once. They had no right to do that. Kalookie was *my* cat, and I should have been asked; I should have been there!!!

I basically went ballistic. The look on my father's face said it all. He was heartbroken and clearly felt terrible, but I kept yelling until I couldn't speak anymore, screaming until I couldn't speak anymore. Then I ran to my room, completely hysterical. Not since I was four years old when my grandparents had died—and at that age I didn't quite get it—had I experienced the death of a loved one. My chest was aching, and it literally felt like my heart had cracked open. My dad came in to comfort me, and I just cried and cried. I couldn't stop. Kalookie had been my constant companion for so many years that I didn't know what I would do without him. He had gotten me through so many times when I had been sick or sad or lonely, and now he was gone—when I needed him most. I finally fell asleep in my bed, very aware of the empty spot next to my head, where we had slept together for years.

So now, even though I was trying to let go of Cleo

like I did Kalookie, I found myself driving up to this apartment, near the infamous dog groomers where Cassandra★ With a Star had dropped Cleo off at the beginning of this quest. The door opened to reveal this large woman with short, cropped hair and pierced body parts.

"*Hi.*"

She stared and quietly uttered, "Wow, you're the chick from *Bound. . . .*"

"*Yes,*" I said, averting my eyes from her stare. "*That would be me. So, where's the cat?*"

She took me around the corner, explaining how this cat had been there for weeks, eating everyone's food, but he wouldn't let anyone touch him. She kept stealing glances at me. I pretended I didn't notice and went into my kitty war cry:

"*HERE, KITTY KITTY. KITTY KITTY! HERE, CLEO! WHERE IS THE CLEO? YOU ARE NO GOOD!*"

Suddenly this savage beast came racing around the corner, wailing with a voice that would rival Harvey Fierstein's. It raced right up to me and started head-butting my leg hard and roaring at me loudly, as if he were saying, "FUCK YOU, FUCK YOU!"

I was a bit taken aback.

The woman with the cropped hair and piercings was shocked.

"That is definitely your cat."

But I wasn't so sure.

Cleo had such a shiny black coat and such a sweet meow. This thing had cuts on his mouth and ears. Mud and crust everywhere. He certainly didn't look or sound like my baby. I reached down to touch him and he ran away, but then he ran back as if he didn't know what to do. I decided, maybe one last time, to take him home and see how things worked out. But I was pretty sure that this cat was not mine.

I pulled out my kitty bag, but he wouldn't come near it. All of a sudden, I heard Sonia's voice in my head: *Dahhhling, he's waiting for the limo.* So I pulled up my Cadillac and he jumped in as soon as I opened the door. I told myself it didn't mean a thing, just another freeloader looking for a ride. I had learned the hard way not to open my heart to a stranger, knowing that it only leads to heartbreak, tears, and weight gain.

We arrived home and the first thing that happened was Luca, the Cleo groupie, who had made me feel like an idiot every time I'd brought home an imposter kitty, came racing over. The beast swatted her away, but Luca would have none of it. She decided that this was indeed Cleo, her lost love.

Promising, but I wasn't gonna get my hopes up. The cat went inside, right to Cleo's now-ceramic bowl and ate a bit, and then he went outside to avoid me. This is something Cleo would do if he was angry with me. This cat even went to Cleo's stone pillar (where Cleo would often go to contemplate life's problems) and sat himself down.

When it was time for bed, I went upstairs, leaving the door open. Eventually the strange cat came upstairs but hardly slept at all because he was too busy cleaning himself. All night long. In the morning, I noticed that the cat on my bed was not the same cat that I had fallen asleep with. His fur was super clean, all black and shiny, and even his cuts were gone, as though he had rid himself of some street disguise and I could look into his bright green eyes for the first time. As our eyes locked, he began cuddling and kissing me, and my heart started to melt when he gave me the sweetest meow ever: *mmrrrrowwww.*

My heart started to pound, and I kept thinking, *Don't get your hopes up.* As I pet his head, I went to his mouth to look inside. He let me. And there it was.

The perfect black dot on the roof of his mouth. I began to hyperventilate. As he went to his water bowl, he looked me straight in the eye, smiled, and BEGAN TO PAW BOTH SIDES OF THE BOWL! Like a horse. Like Cleo. It was him! He was back. I had finally found him. I literally burst into tears! I ran over to him, picked him up, and kissed him and cried and squeezed him so hard he squawked. I literally couldn't believe it. I just could not believe it. We spent the rest of the day in bed together, snuggling and eating tuna . . . juice, meat, and all.

I was so happy, and I thought of Arthur—I had to tell him that I had finally found my baby. He'd be so happy for me! And it would be nice to give him a little something something, a bottle of wine or some money, for his support.

So I woke up the next morning and went to his spot—the spot I'd been to every morning for over two months—but I couldn't find him. No silver Honda, no golden Jheri-curled woman inside filing her nails, no Arthur. Instead, I noticed a teenage Hispanic girl throwing the papers.

"Where's Arthur?"

She didn't answer me.

"Hey! Excuse me. . . . Where's Arthur?"

She turned to me, annoyed.

"Who's Arthur?"

"He's the paper man on this beat."

No reply. She went back to what she was doing.

"Helloooo? Do you where Arthur is?" I asked this time in a more insistent tone.

She finally stopped to look at me.

"I've been working this beat for years, and I never heard of no Arthur."

She turned her back and resumed throwing her papers.

What?!?! I just stood there, dumbfounded into silence, my mind frozen until I remembered to breathe again. I didn't understand. How could that be? This just didn't make any sense. Arthur had been there with me, every step of the way. How could this girl simply say that he hadn't been around? What did she mean? I wanted to tell her that she didn't know what she was talking about. That she was lying. . . . But somehow, I had a strange feeling that she wasn't.

I went back to look for Arthur several times, but I just couldn't find him anywhere. It was as though he just vanished. Like he never even existed. Holy shit. *Holy shit.* What did this mean? I knew I had been poppin' a few dolls and all, but he was *not* a figment

of my imagination. He was definitely real. Unless . . .
What if Arthur was actually my guardian angel?
What if he and his golden girl copilot were the two
spirits that Sonia had told me about? The two spirits
that she said would help me find Cleo? What if the
Twilight Zone was real? What if I had actually lost
my mind? What if, what if, what if??? I didn't have
any answers. I still don't.

I NEVER SAW OR HEARD from Arthur again. I think
about him quite often, though. I hear his words.
His voice. His laugh. He used to tell me that everything happened for a reason. It may not make sense
to us at the time that it's happening, but at some
point, when we have had the time and experience to
look back on our journey, its meaning will be revealed.
Maybe this applies to my past relationships, why they
didn't work out. Perhaps they fell under the old "timing and lighting" theory. Sometimes you can meet
someone and be so attracted to them in so many
ways, but they are still getting over a relationship. Or
they need to go to rehab. Or they simply need to get
their shit together. This would be a case when the
lighting is good, but the timing is off. Or you meet

someone who wants the same things that you do in a relationship and is totally ready and willing to move forward and have a real go at it, but sadly, you aren't attracted to them in that way. At all. This is a case when the timing is good, but the lighting is bad. In either case, the relationship was not meant to be. Hopefully THE person shows up in your life and you think, Thank God the other ones didn't work out! Everything happens for a reason. Many a wise man has expressed this sentiment for centuries in so many words.* I believe it, I've experienced it, and hopefully one day I'll get what this whole journey, this whole search for Cleo, was all about. Because to tell you the truth, at this very moment, I do not understand. Yet.

Afterword

NOT LONG AFTER I FOUND Cleo, I went to Egypt with my Aunt Bobbie. I made sure to find the most reliable and trustworthy cat sitter around. Tess was overweight and unhealthy and thought the word *hippy* referred to fat people, but she adored Cleo, and I knew she would take care of and protect him no matter what. He was in good hands.

Egypt was amazing: the museums, the pyramids, the marketplaces, the music, and the cats. Everywhere I looked there were statues, amulets, pendants, and stories about Bastet, the Egyptian cat goddess, daughter of Ra, the sun god. This goddess represented fertility and pleasure, and she was celebrated in festivals. I asked our Egyptologist about cats, their prevalence, and their mythology. As expected, she told me that they held a very special place among the Egyptians. In ancient times they were deities who protected the family and helped to ward off evil.

"All except the black cat," she pointedly added.

"What do you mean?" I reluctantly asked.

"Well, we believe that the black cat, especially a male black cat, is a dead soul flying around in the universe. And if he spots someone, and falls in love with her, he will come down to earth in the shape of a black cat. A male black cat. And if a male black cat comes to you, and you take him in, YOU WILL NEVER MARRY!" (Cue the ominous, spooky music.)

I told her the story that I just told you, and her eyes widened in fear.

"Get rid of him!!!!" she emphatically implored. "Get rid of him as soon as you get home!! Do not fool around with this! GET RID OF HIM IMMEDIATELY!!!"

Yeah, right. Like that's going to happen.

CLEO AND I have been living in loving bliss ever since his return. As he has gotten older, his black fur has morphed into a brownish white. He's gone from panther to bear. It takes him longer to sit down now and get comfortable. His joints aren't what they used to be. And instead of energetically pawing around his water bowl before he drinks, Cleo gives the floor a few feeble swipes, more out of habit than commitment.

He did have a bout of post-traumatic stress disorder after his ordeal out in the wilds of Los Angeles, but the vet said that that was to be expected after everything he had been through. On top of the PTSD, the vet explained to me that sometimes pets will take on their humans' emotional and physical afflictions. Interesting. Over the past few years, Cleo and I have shared many symptoms. Teeth issues, heart murmurs, intestinal infections, and hyperactive thyroid. Just last year when I was shooting a movie in New Orleans, I had a scene where I got punched in the face. I had fake blood all over me, all day long. It kept dripping into my ear, so I kept shaking my head to get rid of it. Later that day, I got a phone call from my new unfailingly reliable cat nanny, Sarah, who was watching Cleo in Los Angeles. She told me that she had taken him to the vet because he kept shaking his head, and his ear seemed swollen for no apparent reason. The vet, however, couldn't figure out what was wrong. She thought that perhaps he had hit his head or his ear, and while he showed no external signs of bumps or contusions, blood had pooled in his ear and he was trying to get it out.

I know our story, mine and Cleo's, seems implausible. Yet I am here to tell you that it is 96 percent true. Only dates and names have been changed to enhance the drama and to protect the unworthy. As Mark Twain once said, "Truth is stranger than fiction, but it is because Fiction is obliged to stick to possibilities; Truth isn't."

Ain't that the truth.

Index

Page 35: I had the honor of doing a duet with Christian McBride, the most badass jazz bassist living today, on his album *Conversations with Christian*. It's a great album. Buy it today!!!

Page 35: Leroy Powell is an incredible musician and singer (check him out) and he helped me coproduce two records: *In Search of Cleo* and our really fun kids record, *The Good, the Bad, and the Hungry*, by Beardo and Baddo. If you have a kid between the ages of two and ten, or just like to laugh, this album is for you. Hey, this is my book, I can plug my own albums if I want to.

Page 36: Lyrics to "Marie." Check out the song if you are curious about the Jew's harp. Or why not buy the entire album? (Another shameless plug.) Or pirate it with the rest of the world!

>   *Marie*
>   *I looked up from my booster chair*
>   *asked her how she got so tan*
>   *She laughed and said, "I'z a negro child"*
>   *And showed me both sides of her hand.*
>   *Her name was "Marie"*

Met her when I was 2
She bought me salted carrot sticks
As she walked me home from school.
Her family make her pay
When she come to L.A.
So she come to live with me
Told me stories of old and how they'd
     unfold
in Rolling Fork Mississippi.
     Marie
When I was 7 I stole me a box
It had Snoopy playing on The "Boing Boing"
Got in trouble, got caught by a cop
But they never took away my "Boing"
I took that "Boing," put it up to my mouth
til it gave me a blood lip
Marie grabbed it from me and said,
"Child, give me that thing"
and then she made it sound like this . . .
(She say "Geen, Geen child, my cough got worse
     and
I'm getting me a chill, you be a good girl now
and go on to the store and fetch me a big ol'
Bottle of NyQuil." (Another one?))))????
Marie ~Marie

Page 47: Jocelyn Wildenstein is the lady who has had so much plastic surgery that her face looks like a lady cat. You've got to admire her commitment. Hopefully that was her intention. If not, she needs to find a new doctor.

Page 151: Check out Steve Jobs's 2005 Stanford commencement address. It illustrates this idea very eloquently.

Photograph by Robin Davey

In Search of Cleo CD

Thank You

WITH GRATITUDE I'd like to thank the following people who helped me get this crazy story out of my head and onto these pages. Thank you for all of your support and encouragement.

David Kuhn, Lauren Marino, Dann Gershon, James Frey, Rachel Child, Jeff Garlin, Adam McKay, Beardo, Ron Perelman, Steve and Lou Feder-Trosclair, Kristina Bezanis, Alison Spiegel, Deborah Anderson, Zac Posen, Monica Benalcazar, Sam Fishell, Katy Fishell, Ian LeFrenais, Haley Alexander van Oosten. And my Baba.

And a heartfelt thank-you to my friends and family and strangers who helped me keep my sanity and hold my hand during the time that I was looking for Cleo. I could not have made it through without your love and support. Thank you.

Lonnye Bower; Denis Leary; Ellen DeGeneres; Amanda Demme; my sister, Tracy; my brother, Dann; my mom; Tanta; Joanna Elliot; Rick Rubin; Kevin Hunter; and Arthur . . . wherever you are.

Part of *In Search of Cleo*'s proceeds will be given to these excellent animal organizations that are close to my heart.

If you aren't already aware of the amazing work that these foundations do, please take a moment to check them out.

Many thanks to . . .

Green Chimneys
The Lange Foundation
Pets Alive Animal Sanctuary
North Shore Animal League